Praise for *Leadersh...*

CW01508440

"If you're advancing in your ⟨...⟩ ...ps you shape the leader you want to be. If you're earlier in your career, this book helps you shape the role work plays in your life. This read is for all who seek a purposeful paycheck."

– Donna Peters, Founder of The Me-Suite and author of *Options Are Power*

"I had just stepped into my new role as manager when I picked up this book, and it couldn't have come at a better time. Instead of me trying to be the 'perfect' traditional manager, this book helped me to see how being true to myself would lead me to be the right manager for my team. It's refreshing to read about kindness and values in the corporate world as strengths rather than weaknesses, and I'm grateful for Janice's insight into how to be a successful manager in today's corporate environment."

– Talysa Sainz, Underwriting Manager at MotivHealth

"Janice Jackson presents a compelling examination of corporate leadership challenges and offers practical advice on how to break the cycle of the past and become the servant leader needed for today's modern workplace. Each chapter brims with insights that challenge conventional wisdom, offering transformative tips on navigating patriarchy, embracing authenticity, and showing that kindness in leadership is a powerful tool for maintaining authority, building dynamic teams, and driving exceptional results.

Overall, the book is a comprehensive guide to modern leadership, calling for outdated practices to be replaced with a more inspiring, authentic and empathetic approach. Each chapter builds on the previous one, creating a well-rounded and practical resource for current and aspiring leaders. A good read that is timely and relevant, particularly when corporate America is in need of more women leaders."

– Jamie O'Born, CEO of The Printing House Ltd

"Having worked for Janice myself, let me validate that she is the real deal. All of the best practices, leadership advice and guiding principles outlined in her book are a direct reflection of her leadership. If you want to truly level up your own ability to lead others and stay true to yourself authentically, this is a must-read!

My personal favorites are around managing yourself around challenging bosses and peers, dodging the patriarchy pitfalls and never settling. We walked through some difficult times together and her guidance was my lifeline. Read the book and share it with others in your circle!"

– Kristina Swift, Owner, Serendipity Executive Search

"I read the book and it made me understand that I have worked in small, medium and large organisations in my career and encountered bad leadership in all of these. Every time I moved on from a job it was in response to bosses—always male—who ran businesses without having any management training and really didn't know what they were doing! By the time I was the leader, I hope I was the right kind...This book is a handbook for all aspiring leaders, but especially female ones. You have clearly put a great deal of thought into the causes of poor leadership and come up with really useful advice on how to make change happen. I particularly liked the phrase 'you do not need perfection to happen for excellence to occur.' So many women, both at home and in the workplace, strive so hard for perfection that they fail to appreciate their own excellence! This book could change that!"

– Julia Hunter, Optometry Specialist, formerly with the United Kingdom National Health Service

LEADERSHIP MATTERS

LEADERSHIP MATTERS

It's Time for Good Leaders
to Outnumber the Bad.
The Change Starts with You.

Janice Jackson

Leadership Matters: It's Time for the Good Leaders to Outnumber the Bad
Published by Jackspublishing LLC
Belmont, Michigan, U.S.A.

JACKSON, JANICE, Author
LEADERSHIP MATTERS
JANICE JACKSON

Library of Congress Control Number: 2024911785

ISBN: 979-8-9908388-0-2, 979-8-9908388-2-6 (paperback)
ISBN: 979-8-9908388-3-3 (hardcover)
ISBN: 979-8-9908388-1-9 (digital)

BUSINESS & ECONOMICS / Leadership
BODY, MIND & SPIRIT / Inspiration & Personal Growth
SELF-HELP / Personal Growth / Success
BUSINESS & ECONOMICS / Organizational Development

QUANTITY PURCHASES: Schools, companies, professional groups, clubs, and other organizations may qualify for special terms when ordering quantities of this title. For information, email jackspublishing44@gmail.com

To those who want to evolve and grow as leaders,
and stand their ground
when faced with incompetent and toxic bosses.

Table of Contents

Introduction

L eadership quality in the corporate world has taken a nosedive. It seems as if there are "horrible bosses" around every corner! And I can guarantee you have felt the same. How often do you hear about the nightmare CEO or the overdemanding supervisor? How often have you had one yourself?

Every person I know has experienced a boss, or even multiple bosses, who have squashed their dreams, belittled them, or worked them so hard they burned out. Horrible bosses can do a lot of damage and undo a lot of development. It's unacceptable. And it shouldn't happen. But it does, every single day. It leaves direct reports and entire teams feeling uninspired, and it makes companies flounder without understanding why.

And it doesn't just suck for those being managed. Leaders also often find themselves looking in the mirror and thinking, "Who the hell is that?" The "horrible boss" they see staring back at them doesn't resonate with their true self. Behind the public face and polished persona, there's a deeply rooted fear. A fear of rejection, a fear of not getting respect, a fear of doing something wrong—or, worse, a fear of failing.

This fear is a cocktail of past experiences, bad power dynamics, and cues taken from the wrong role models. Many leaders today have been under the thumb of overpowering superiors in the past. When they finally get a taste of "power," instead of being the change they would love to have seen when they were younger, they perpetuate the cycle and wield their newfound authority like a sledgehammer.

This is not the behavior of evolved, responsible adults. These are the actions of individuals enslaved by their past, by their misperceptions, and by their insecurities. Blindly wearing the mask of what they think real leaders should look like: egotistical, unapproachable, and sometimes downright arrogant.

But *YOU* don't have to lead this way.

Right now, there is a desperate need for corporate leaders to break this mold. To strip away the mask and be approachable, empathetic, open, kind, and coachable. But many corporate leaders today don't know how to get there.

I've seen some of the good, and a lot of the bad and the ugly, of corporate leadership. I've seen too many leaders trapped in preconceived notions of what leadership should look like.

My leadership approach is rooted in authenticity, humanity, and servant leadership. I've poured my heart into developing every team member I've worked with. When describing my leadership style, most of my direct reports have used phrases like "breath of fresh air," "empowering," "authentic," and "opened my eyes to my own potential." If there's one facet of leadership that I hold dearest, it's nurturing talent. Seeing individuals flourish, evolve, and truly come into their own is the most gratifying experience. The legacy I hope to leave behind is a line of leaders who echo the same values and pay it forward. This is the type of evolved leadership that always leads to excellent performance and results. And this is the type of leader I will teach you how to become in this book.

Shockingly, genuine investment in talent remains, in my opinion, a rarity in the corporate world. I aim to change that depressing reality. I have seen the damage the plague of "horrible bosses" inflicts. I want to put an end to it.

Of course, there *are* good leaders out there. But they are few and far between, and the majority of corporate leaders are miserably failing those in their charge. The ripple effects of a single misguided leader can impact so many lives, dreams, and aspirations, leaving employees demoralized, drowning in criticism, and unable to reach their full potential. Despite an overwhelming supply of tools, courses, and resources designed to mold the *ideal* leader, we seem to be stuck using outdated leadership tactics that disenfranchise, demotivate, and dehumanize our teams.

My journey through the corporate maze has been far from smooth. More often than not, I found myself confronted with leadership that lacked vision, empathy, and integrity. Each encounter left a mark. The bumps and bruises from these run-ins became constant reminders of the uphill battle many face in the corporate world, making me even more determined to do better myself and teach others to do the same.

I wrote this book to offer guidance to corporate leaders or aspiring leaders who don't know how to break the norms of the leaders before them. It is filled to the brim with strategies I used to make a difference in the lives of those I led. Throughout my career, I'm proud to say I know of no one who has worked with me who wouldn't do so again.

If you want to say that about your leadership career, and more importantly, your legacy, keep reading.

Chapter 1:

Recognize That Most Corporate Leadership Sucks

That first step into the corporate world is a monumental transition. Think about the first job you had. Were you nervous? Did you hope to make a difference? Did you have big dreams of climbing the ladder? In the first moments we enter the corporate world, we are lit up with enthusiasm, and, equipped with our new academic credentials, we anticipate a workplace where we can contribute meaningfully.

Unfortunately, we often experience anything but welcoming, inspiring, and innovative leaders.

Any young adult fresh out of university is filled with a "you can change the world" attitude. They have worked countless hours to gain the qualifications they need to enter the professional workplace. They might also have gained experience with internships, volunteer work, and part-time gigs. And through their education, they have been trained to question norms, to think critically, and to look outside the box for innovative solutions. But the corporate world so often doesn't want them to do any of that.

Instead, when many of these bright young professionals start their first jobs, they find themselves shut down, cut off, and ignored by seasoned professionals who are looking to defend their turf. Which leaves new entrants with the stark realization that they are at the bottom of the food chain, and their aspirations of making a tangible impact are quickly squashed. If you have been there (as too many of us have), I'm truly sorry. This experience is one of the quickest ways many of us become demotivated because it's so confusing! Modern business practices tell us we should encourage and share new insights, but instead, we are met with a hierarchical wall that seems to defy the very principles of modern business practices and a to-do list nobody wants you to question.

To put it plainly, many of us are treated like children in our first job. We are expected to perform tasks without question, and we are constantly monitored or ignored to exhaustion.

The stereotypical leaders who, instead of nurturing talent, squash it under the weight of their egos and old-school management styles, believe in dictation rather than dialogue and micro-management instead of empowerment. This approach is debilitating to any individual and will likely stifle creativity and enthusiasm. Which means many industries miss out on game-changing ideas and the innovation they so desperately need.

Think about the untapped potential, the fresh perspectives, and the innovative solutions that have never seen the light of day. How much do you think we have lost in innovation because of this? I think it's probably a lot! When I had bad leaders, I never felt comfortable sharing my ideas or perspectives with them. And you have likely felt the same way at one point or another. When employees are treated as cogs in the machine, the machine becomes outdated, stagnant, and uncompetitive.

And that sucks!

Unfortunately, many of us have experienced this from day one. This type of leadership takes a deep, personal toll on each of us. We begin to question our worth. We start to believe (wrongly) that maybe *we* are the problem. Our dreams and aspirations are replaced by doubt, and we start to think to ourselves, "Maybe I'm not cut out for this," or "Maybe this is my fault."

But the truth is it's often not us. It is the environment, the leadership, and the systemic issues that create uninspiring and unevolved leaders who feel like they have to lead like those who came before them in order to keep their job. This toxic cycle kicks the hell out of all of us.

Disengagement Is Rampant

When corporate leadership stifles creativity, employees who once brimmed with enthusiasm find themselves gradually sapped of motivation. Nobody performs well under those circumstances. In the absence of an inspiring figure who can guide and motivate, these individuals are left feeling disengaged.

Each one of us has likely experienced this in real life. I know I have. I recently observed a talented employee within the creative department of a mid-sized company who became increasingly disenchanted and exhausted. She was dealing with a "leader" with no leadership skills who continually changed directions and required constant re-work from her. Which meant this previously engaged and enthusiastic employee no longer speaks up in meetings because she knows the work and time she puts in is completely disregarded.

Recent data further illuminates this issue and points to an alarming trend. According to a recent Gallup study[1], employee engagement in the U.S. continues to decline, with only 32% of full- and part-time employees currently engaged. Worse yet, 17% are actively disengaged. This decline started in late 2021, and further studies show the trend getting worse, with employees increasingly feeling disconnected from their roles and the broader objectives of their organizations.

Engaged employees—as identified by the study—are those who are genuinely involved in, enthusiastic about, and committed to their work and workplace. They are the individuals who are most likely to drive innovation, create value, and build vital bridges with customers. On the flip side, actively disengaged employees are not just unhappy at work; they are resentful that their potential is not being tapped and, as a result, act out this unhappiness. These employees are more likely to "quietly quit," performing the bare minimum amount of work, negatively influencing coworkers, skipping workdays, and driving customers away.

What leads to these levels of disengagement? Poor leadership! It's leadership that sets the tone, establishes the expectations, and fosters (or suppresses) an environment conducive to growth and

---

1 (Harter, 2022)

development. These historic levels of disengagement should be a wake-up call for leaders and companies everywhere. Despite clear evidence pointing to the need for change, many in leadership roles remain stubbornly entrenched in outdated modes. They continue to operate with a narrow focus on short-term goals and immediate outputs, often at the cost of long-term employee engagement and development.

True leadership is about more than driving results; it's about nurturing talent, encouraging personal and professional growth, and creating a culture where employees feel valued and understood. Leaders who fail to recognize this are not just failing their teams; they are also failing their organizations.

This becomes even worse for A-players. A-players, or star performers who are typically reliable and exhibit high levels of productivity, are often tasked with heavier workloads and higher expectations. They bear the brunt of team responsibilities while observing less committed (or disengaged) team members not pulling their weight. Without any intervention from leadership, resentment builds, and burnout becomes a reality. Which means even A-players can become quickly disengaged, leaving clueless leadership wondering what happened to their motivation. Have you ever been an A-player on a team? I'm curious—how long was it before you became overwhelmed with work?

Mismanagement Snuffs Out Passion

I had the privilege of coaching a bright millennial woman who is a digital marketing expert. Her talents, especially in our digital world, are naturally in high demand. Companies are clamoring for her expertise, and she constantly receives interesting and high-paying job opportunities. However, to date, she has rarely found the type of leadership she hopes to learn from and be inspired by.

Twice, she has joined companies who promised her the world: empowerment, a chance to truly utilize her talent, and a workplace that respects work-life balance. They told her, "We're like one big family," and assured her she would be valued in the position.

And, twice, she found herself walking into a maelstrom.

The chaos didn't come only from her workload; it came from the lack of clear leadership. Directions were like arrows fired from multiple bows, often conflicting, and sometimes even contradictory. There was no clear decision-making tree. The excitement of putting processes in place and streamlining operations quickly gave way to the fatigue of navigating murky waters, dodging conflicting directions, and endlessly revisiting work she had already perfected.

Turns out, the promise of work-life balance was a mirage. The "family" they spoke of felt more like a dysfunctional one. And as an A-player, she was constantly overworked and under-informed for the work she was expected to do. Because of all this, her sense of accomplishment was almost gone. Repeatedly, the final product she would deliver was misdirected or diluted to such an extent that it devolved into a shadow of what she could have achieved in a more structured, focused environment.

It was heartbreaking to see, and she came to me for advice. Here was a company pouring significant resources into acquiring a gem, only to keep her brilliance buried under layers of disorganization and lack of vision. For someone so deeply committed to her craft, this was soul-crushing. The toll it took on her spirit made her doubt her worth and question whether she was cut out for the work.

Unfortunately, almost all of us have experienced something like this in the corporate world. What did you feel when your ideas were squashed by a superior? How did it affect your work moving forward? Did you continue to bring ideas to the table, or did you eventually just go with whatever leaders said they wanted?

When we pause to answer these questions and look back on our own experiences in the corporate world, it often stirs a deep sense of frustration and anger. We see our own lost potential. To that I say, good! I hope you get angry. I hope you get so angry that you work to become a leader who makes sure others don't experience the same soul-crushing heartache you have. Bad management will always snuff out passion, and none of us (new entrants or seasoned workers) deserve to have our potential snuffed out.

What was my advice to this young woman? Get out. Get out before your motivation and enthusiasm is smothered entirely. There are companies out there—though they are sadly few and hard to find—with enlightened leadership who recognize, respect, and reward talent like hers. Sometimes the best move you can make is to find a place that actually values your worth. No paycheck or title can compensate for a workplace that diminishes your light.

Every individual thrives when they feel seen, acknowledged, and valued. When a professional's expertise goes unrecognized, it isn't just their immediate output that suffers, but their long-term enthusiasm and motivation as well. Over time, the enthusiastic spark that once drove them to innovate and excel dwindles, potentially even extinguishing their passion for their field entirely.

Corporate vs. Entrepreneurship

For countless individuals, the allure of the corporate world holds a promise of stability, a chance to be a part of a dynamic team, and an opportunity to climb the professional ladder. These are the individuals who, by choice, don't dream of starting their own businesses. Instead, they are excited to be part of something larger and to thrive within the structure of a well-defined role and a collaborative team.

However, when they are not met with inspired, high-functioning teams, but instead are thrust into a sea of ill-equipped leadership that starts stripping away at the core of who they are, the corporate world doesn't seem like such a good idea. Where does that leave them? Stuck between corporate leaders who resort to undermining tactics, power plays, and mind games—or entrepreneurship, where you are often alone and the success of everything is entirely up to you.

For many today, the struggle of entrepreneurship seems more attractive and less soul-crushing than the current corporate world. These people often leave corporate life and try their hand at building a business on their own. Though many sing the praises of starting one's own business, the truth is, it's not for everyone. Some individuals don't have the appetite for the uncertainties that come with entrepreneurship. Others deeply value the social interactions and team dynamics of corporate settings. They cherish the brainstorming sessions, the group projects, and the collective sense of achievement.

Which makes this route of going it alone—that they have been forced to try—less than ideal.

The decision between embarking on an entrepreneurial journey versus joining the corporate world should be clear-cut, based purely on individual aspirations, risk tolerance, and personality. However, the current state of corporate leadership is pushing many off their chosen paths and making them question their place in the corporate realm. This only adds to the amount of people leaving the workplace today.

There is a common misconception that "people don't want to work." I'd argue it's not that they don't want to work—it's that they don't want to work for terrible leaders.

The Leadership Struggle

Those being managed aren't the only ones struggling. Corporate leadership faces its own set of challenges, many of which stem from societal and historical precedents about what leadership should look like.

If you are already a leader, you know *exactly* what I'm talking about. You have likely been managed by someone who is unapproachable and the opposite of encouraging. Which means when it's your turn to take the wheel, you feel you have to do the same. Sadly, the only role models many individuals encounter have been so poor that they feel the need to diminish others as they were once diminished.

It's a vicious cycle, and it won't stop unless we actively work to change it.

For centuries, leaders have been depicted as strong, authoritative, and unyielding figures. From monarchs to military generals, the image of a leader is an ironclad individual, impervious to emotions and personal struggles. This image places a huge burden on contemporary leaders, many of whom feel pressured to live up to this archetype, which means suppressing vulnerability and hesitating to show emotions. In fact, PwC, (PricewaterhouseCoopers), did a study on the fears and hopes of the global workforce, and in that study, they found 33% of the respondents said "their manager encourages dissent and debate," still opting for the classic divide and conquer approach[2].

Why does this happen?

Many leaders ascend to their positions without adequate coaching or mentorship. This leaves them to copy what they have seen other leaders do because they don't have a solid grounding in leadership principles or strategies. If these observed behaviors were negative or abusive, the new leaders might inadvertently

---

2 (PwC, 2023)

perpetuate them simply because they don't know another way. The weight of decisions, the distance from on-the-ground realities, and the layers of bureaucracy further remove leaders from the very people they are supposed to guide.

The worst part is that many of these leaders don't like what they are doing. They see the extent to which people are demotivated by their behavior, but they don't know another way. Becoming a leader who impacts others for good requires an intentionality and vulnerability that is daunting. I wish I could tell you it isn't, but it is. It requires self-awareness, self-confidence, and self-esteem as well as the understanding that you are there to lift those who you lead. All things which don't often come to us naturally.

Our C-suite leaders at the helm should be committed to ensuring that the leaders within their organizations are equipped with the emotional intelligence as well as the technical expertise they need to do the job well. This evolved approach to leadership will help modern leaders stop struggling themselves and prevent them from damaging the careers and lives of all around them.

What Next?

Corporate leadership sucks in many ways I've covered in this chapter and in many other ways I haven't covered. But we can't let this be the norm any longer. True power doesn't come from authority. It comes from lifting up those we lead.

My goal is to arm you with insights, strategies, and real-world examples that act as a roadmap for change. If you've felt the agony of lost potential and the frustration of stifled innovation, then you are already ahead of the curve. You recognize the problem.

This book is your guide to becoming part of the solution.

Chapter Wrap Up

As you analyze the current corporate leadership surrounding you, remember that:

- Too often, those who are just starting in the corporate world are met with leaders who believe in micro-management instead of empowerment.
- Disengaged employees are a direct result of poor leadership.
- Mismanagement is one of the quickest ways to snuff out employee passion.
- Many A-players, who want to work for a corporation, are being forced to move from the corporate world into the entrepreneurial world because of poor leadership.
- Many leaders in the world today are struggling but don't know how to change their leadership style.

If you recognize these problems, you are ready to become a better leader and to stand your ground when faced with a terrible boss.

Chapter 2:

Remove the Mask

A ccording to a recent Gallup study[3], 50% of employees leave their jobs to get away from a bad leader. This was in spite of good pay, the role being a good fit, and even high passion for the company. Bad managers are one of the biggest reasons people leave their jobs today.

I bet reading that statistic made you think of a bad leader in your life. Someone who has pushed you down, hampered your joy, or even made you quit your job to get away from them. These leaders are often not genuine or authentic, and you as the employee can sense it. This lack of authenticity can erode trust in the leader. Especially if they wear a mask and project an image that is not who they truly are. Their words feel insecure, they lack conviction, and their actions often seem out of sync with their professed values.

Unfortunately, many leaders in the corporate world do wear a mask. They feel they *have* to, due to the perceived expectations and pressures associated with their roles. They might even believe that to command respect, maintain authority, or project an image

---

3 (Nolan, n.d.)

of unflappable confidence, they need to consistently project a certain persona. Even if that persona doesn't entirely align with their true selves.

Many leaders fear that revealing their genuine emotions, uncertainties, or weaknesses could lead to judgments from their boss or diminish their authority in the eyes of their team. And industry norms or past experiences might have conditioned them to think that authentic leadership is synonymous with being unprofessional or too emotionally involved. This is old-school! This is the old story many of us, leaders or not, were taught as we grew up. And because of this, it is too easy for our authentic selves to be overshadowed by the roles we feel we are expected to play in the corporate world.

I know, I've seen it. There were times, when I started out, that I was tempted to follow these norms. Leadership roles seem to come with their own set of rules, expectations, and even scripted dialogues. The expectation to conform to these norms is overwhelming, especially when you are new to leadership and are unsure how you should manage others.

But the thing is, leaders who wear a mask are profoundly frustrating for those managed by them. They present a façade employees can sense. They never reveal their true feelings, thoughts, or intentions, and they put employees on edge. Especially if they feel they don't truly know who their leader is and how they might react to complex or high-stress situations. As a result, employees are left trying to decipher the real motivations and priorities behind their manager's actions. This breeds a sense of insecurity and mistrust in the workplace. Team members constantly feel like they are walking on eggshells, unsure of where they stand or what's genuinely expected of them.

In that scenario, would you want to speak up and ask questions or provide an opinion? If you're shaking your head no, trust me, I wouldn't want to either. When leaders hide behind masks, they inadvertently create barriers that can stymie both individual growth and collective success. Employees may hesitate to share their concerns or ideas, fearing potential hidden agendas or repercussions. They might also struggle to connect on a personal level with a leader who doesn't show their true self, making it harder to foster genuine rapport and mutual respect.

If you are a leader, I want you to ask yourself: Beneath the armor, the carefully crafted LinkedIn profiles, and the professional jargon—who are you really?

The answer to this question is critical. Not just for your own sense of self, but for better connections with your team. You have to remove the mask and understand yourself before you can be effective.

Here is a trick you can use to stay on track:

1. Think about a person who has profoundly impacted your life—a favorite teacher, a loving parent, a supportive coach, or an inspirational boss. Someone who you want to be like.

2. Ask yourself, would this person recognize you in your role? Would your actions make them proud? Aligning your actions with what would make them proud acts

as an internal compass and helps you stay true to your values.

Self-reflection is the best way to remove the mask. Knowing who you are, accepting it, and acting in harmony with your true self is the most evolved form of leadership there is. In order to do any of that, you first have to remove the mask and shed any preconceived notions you might have about what a leader *should* be.

Self-Reflection Is the Gateway to Authentic Leadership

Before you can effectively lead a team, you have to know yourself.

Think about one of the best experiences you have ever had on a team. What was this like? What actions went into creating the team? What effort went into ensuring open communication and a safe space context for the team? What results came from this team? Did you feel euphoria when the goal was achieved? Are you still connected with those on the team, even if you have moved on?

For many, a good team experience typically occurs during their leisure time, such as sports, a trivia team, or a club. But it is possible to experience this type of highly functioning and highly satisfying team in the workplace as well.

This *should* be part of every corporate experience. Sadly, it very often isn't.

Leaders who excel in their roles create spaces where team members feel valued, heard, and inspired to contribute their best work. From my experience, this elevates the team and the entire organization, which makes these types of leaders invaluable. Especially when exceptional teams lead to higher employee satisfaction, stronger client relationships, and enhanced profitability for the entire organization.

Unfortunately, many corporations *hope* to find excellent leaders but don't know how to cultivate these leaders. They provide generic leadership training that isn't focused on *how* to lead but what admin tasks are required of a leader. They frequently promote individuals into leadership positions because of tenure or tactical skill sets and not because of their ability to inspire. Then they often ignore skills like personal development, people management, and emotional intelligence. This blatant neglect in the quality of leadership leaves managers, directors, vice presidents, and C-suite leaders scrambling.

However, there are rare corporate leader gems who do it right.

In the book *American Icon* by Bryce G. Hoffman[4], we get a sneak peek into the fight to save Ford Motor Company during the Great Recession. Bill Ford hired Alan Mullaly as CEO because he believed his "leadership genius" would be a last chance to save the iconic motor company that was losing $6B a quarter. And boy did Alan shake things up. He knew nothing about building cars, having come from the aeronautics industry, but he did know how to manage and inspire people. Under his leadership, Alan moved Ford from bankruptcy to a global powerhouse without resorting to the federal bailouts given to their competitors.

---

4 (Hoffman, 2013)

Alan turned out to be the leader Ford needed. He would commonly say, "The help will never come from a particular place, it will come from yourself." He was an evolved and exceptional leader because he was authentic and held himself to the highest standards. He was empathetic, focused, and had the ability to inspire.

You have to ask yourself where Ford would be today without Alan's guidance.

More notable leaders out there who have punched through the corporate leadership norms include Tim Cook from Apple, Sheryl Sandberg from Facebook, Mary Barra from GM, Jack Ma from Alibaba, and Reshma Saujani from Girls Who Code. These are all incredible leaders who have leaned into their talents and honed their ability to connect with their teams. And let me let you in on a little secret. Though all of these leaders come from several different industries, they have one thing in common: They don't pretend to be anyone other than who they are.

Before they could inspire anyone, they had to get to know themselves. They had to have a solid understanding of who they were and what values drove them, and they had to figure out how they could leverage their strengths to mitigate their weaknesses and support every individual in their team.

What do you stand for? If you can't answer that question, how can you expect to lead others? Leadership involves navigating a sea of differing opinions, behaviors, and challenges. The only way to steer the ship successfully is to have a firm grasp on your understanding of who you are and what you value.

Define the Leader You Want to Be

Gallup's State of the American Manager report[5] studied 2.5 million teams across 195 countries. They found most people became managers because they were either promoted due to success in their role, or they had experience and tenure in their company. If you are in this same boat, like many leaders are, it's time to dig deeper into the type of leader you want to be. To figure out your core values, start by asking yourself these questions:

- Who do you admire most in the world? It could be anyone from a famous figure to your mom, dad, or an elementary school teacher.
- Why do you admire them?
- How would you like to be treated?
- Why do you want to be treated this way? (For example, you might value trust and therefore want to be a trustworthy person.)

Next, think about your professional experiences:

- Recall a time when you felt the most fulfilled at work. Why did you feel that way?
- Think about a time you felt let down or unsupported at work. What led to those feelings?
- Remember a time you experienced significant success professionally. What factors contributed to that success? Often, it's not just your own efforts, but the support, trust, and guidance of others that make the difference.

---

5 (Gallup, n.d.)

Based on the answers to these questions, create a list of the core values that are most important to you. This list of core values becomes instrumental in shaping your leadership style. By leading with a clear understanding and unwavering commitment to these values, you not only strengthen your leadership identity but also set a clear example for others.

The most charismatic and inspiring leader you know likely has this figured out. They operate from a place of genuine understanding and alignment with their own values, and it's part of what makes them inspiring. Because this alignment has a powerful ripple effect. People are naturally drawn to leaders who are true to themselves and their beliefs. When your team members or colleagues see that your actions are consistently aligned with your stated values, it builds trust and respect.

Once you know the answers to these questions and have a better understanding of who you are, it's time to integrate your values into your leadership style. Start by consistently making decisions that align with these values and communicate these values to your team, making them a foundation for team culture and expectations. Encourage open discussions where team members can share their own values and see how they align with or complement the broader organizational ethos. When faced with challenges or dilemmas, revert to these core values as a compass to guide your actions and decisions.

Think of your values as a blueprint for your team. They get to see not just what you're doing, but why you're doing it. And it's that "why" part that really clicks with people. It's what fires them up to buy into the team's vision and your leadership. When you are clear about who you are, you become the kind of leader people are genuinely thrilled to follow.

If you still need a bit more help defining who you are, check out these books which have helped shape my own leadership style:

1. *Daring Greatly* by Brené Brown
2. This book explores the power of vulnerability in various aspects of life, including leadership. Brené Brown argues that embracing vulnerability can lead to stronger relationships, more courage, and a deeper sense of purpose.
3. *Your Survival Strategies Are Killing You* by Martha Borst
4. Martha Borst outlines eight principles that, when adopted, can lead to thriving both professionally and personally. This book is especially helpful for those who feel stuck or restrained by their current approach to challenges.
5. *The Art of Possibility* by Rosamund Stone Zander
6. This book provides a fresh perspective on how to transform your professional and personal life. Zander shares frameworks and stories that inspire a more optimistic and creative mindset.
7. *Be* by Jessica Zweig
8. This book serves as a straightforward guide to enhancing your self-worth and, as a result, your net worth. Zweig argues that authenticity is the key to a fulfilling and successful life.

And finally, if you like a good training course, check out Martha Borst's Personal and Professional Development Training. I've attended her self-mastery courses—both basic and advanced—and have sent my direct reports as well as entire teams to her workshops. Topics range from self-mastery to conflict resolution, team building, and purpose setting. They are well worth your time.

There are countless other books and courses tailored to fit different preferences and needs. However, the most important step is taking action—investing in self-reflection is an investment in your leadership capabilities.

Assessment Tools Should Be More Than a Fun Exercise

If you want to become a leader who inspires others, self-awareness is a must. In my opinion, personal assessment tools are a great way to start. They can help you understand yourself, hone your leadership skills, and understand each individual member of your team so you can better support their development.

I recommend using a tool like DiSC to help you. Based on William Moulton Marston's model of behavior theory[6], the DiSC assessment aids individuals in understanding their behavior, communication styles, and what motivates them. It is designed to evaluate four primary behavioral traits, each of which contains personal strengths and weaknesses: Dominance (D), Influence (I), Steadiness (S), and Conscientiousness (C). I have used DiSC

---

6 (DiSC, n.d.)

assessments multiple times throughout my career across various leadership positions, and each time, it has worked wonders.

One key instance that comes to mind. When I was in the midst of a much-needed company-wide restructuring, I was tasked with setting up a new division. This division would be formed after a round of layoffs (which nobody enjoys).

These situations are emotionally and strategically complex. Job loss creates an emotional toll on leaders and employees. Those who make the cut to stay might even experience survivor's guilt. It isn't exactly a breeding ground for innovation or excitement (neither should it be). Workflow, culture, and company dynamics were about to take a dramatic hit. And I was expected to build and motivate a team.

I knew I had an obligation to handle this situation with as much integrity and empathy as possible. As the layoffs started, we ensured each person affected received an explanation as to why their role was changing and what their strengths were. They then received references for new positions. The gravity of the situation was immense, and the survival of the company was at stake. But we worked hard to make sure every person we parted with was treated with dignity and set up for success at their next position.

Then it was time to tackle the new division. Those who made the cut had appreciated and respected how we handled the layoffs because we made sure no one left the building without a way to move forward. This consideration significantly increased the focus and interest they had in the development of this new division.

I know my DiSC profile. I am an ID, which stands for Influencer-Dominant. But I didn't know the DiSC profiles of those who were about to join this division. So, I asked them to take the assessment and send me their results. As I looked at my pool of marketers and salespeople, many   shared the ID or DI behavioral style—people prone to taking charge and pushing ahead. While this can be an asset, I knew the leadership team of this division should be balanced to avoid blind spots and ensure diverse problem-solving approaches. If you have a leadership team full of similar styles, you will likely miss out on great ideas and unique insights as well as critical checks and balances.

So, I took a different path. I prioritized selecting leads for Supply Chain, Legal, and Finance who frequently had S and C as the lead styles in their DiSC profiles. S stands for Steadiness—the people who are the glue that keeps the team together, who appreciate the nuances of tradition and are cautious when adopting new directions. C stands for Conscientiousness—the analyzers and calculators, the ones who want all the facts before making a decision. By assembling a leadership team with a mix of Ds, Is, Ss, and Cs, I was intentionally crafting a more balanced, effective, and agile team.

Now, I'm not saying any part of this situation was easy. In fact, it's a situation many companies find themselves in and, during the process, lose the respect of their employees. However, by understanding our employees' behavioral styles and preferences and strategically placing the right people in suitable roles, we changed a challenging situation into a positive outcome. We ensured all those involved felt respected.

Unfortunately, many companies introduce the DiSC assessment (or other personality assessments) as a sort of team-building exercise and then never leverage their potential. Almost as if these assessments are a momentary distraction of fun before they want their employees to "get back to work." What a missed opportunity! DiSC, or any other assessment used in your company, should be more than a fun get-to-know-you exercise which quickly gets shelved and forgotten. It is strategic and insightful information. And this information can be used for assembling, understanding, and building cohesive teams.

When leaders and companies use tools like DiSC intentionally, they set a stage to identify and promote individuals who should *genuinely* be in leadership positions. These are the people who can harness diverse talents and perspectives within a team, guiding them to collective success. By focusing on these qualities, organizations are more likely to place people in leadership roles who should actually be there.

Should You Be a Leader?

Part of removing the mask is truthfully asking yourself if you are the type of person who *should* be a leader.

Some people want leadership positions but shouldn't have them. Many crave these positions for the wrong reasons. Ironically, the individuals most eager to climb the managerial ladder are often the least qualified because of skewed motivations. They're driven by status, ambition, and a desire for power over others, not by a genuine wish to foster team growth or contribute to collective goals.

So how do you spot those who shouldn't be leaders? And how do you recognize if you aren't cut out to be a leader yourself?

I remember being at a hyper-growth company, working against the clock with a dedicated team to revamp a floor in our head office. The schedule was tight, and we had builders on site, ready to transform the space. Our team was in constant motion, brainstorming and swiftly tackling challenges during the construction process. At the same time, we were ensuring that the company's daily operations didn't skip a beat.

In the midst of this hectic environment, one of my ten directors seemed to have different priorities. Instead of focusing on the critical tasks at hand, he was fixated on his parking space. Repeatedly, he approached me—bypassing pressing discussions and crucial decision-making moments—to inquire about where he would park his car. He wanted a spot that was sizable and located near the founder's parking spot.

Here we were, in the thick of a significant project, where each team member's contribution was vital to our success. Yet, this director was preoccupied with a personal status symbol.

His actions spoke volumes about his leadership qualities, or lack thereof. It became increasingly clear that his priorities were misaligned with the values and objectives of the team and the company. Talk about a glaring red flag! This was a classic sign that he was more interested in himself than in the well-being of the collective unit.

Many of us have aspired to leadership positions for the wrong reasons at some point in our lives. Often, we pursue these roles because they seem to be one of the only options for upward mobility. This is an understandable misconception in a world where leadership roles are frequently equated with higher status, better pay, and more influence.

But true leadership is about more than just a title or a means to personal advancement. It's the commitment to nurture and elevate those you lead. It involves being invested in the growth and success of your team members. A genuine leader sees their role not just as a manager of tasks, but as a mentor, a coach, and a supporter who helps unlock the potential of their team.

If your ambitions in seeking a leadership position do not include a deep-seated commitment to the development and well-being of your team, then perhaps management isn't the right path for you. Leadership should be a selfless act, where the growth of the team and the realization of their collective goals become your priority, far surpassing personal accolades.

Chapter Wrap Up

When removing the mask, remember:
- Many poor leaders feel they have to wear a mask due to perceived expectations and leadership norms.
- You have to know exactly who you are before you effectively lead a team.
- Be clear in defining your core leadership values and live by them.

- Don't be afraid to use assessment tools for you and your team members to become more self-aware.
- Part of removing the mask is accepting whether or not you are meant to be a leader.
- Make the conscious choice to remove your mask, even when other leaders around you continue to wear theirs.

Chapter 3:

Focus on How You Come Across to Others

We have all heard the phrase, "You have seven seconds to make a first impression." And the Association for Psychological Science argues it could be even fewer[7]. But when we think of this stat, it's usually aligned with branding, job interviews, or even a first date. We don't often associate these first impressions with our communication styles or think about how they might affect the way we lead.

We are all partly products of our upbringing, and these factors shape how we communicate and interact in professional settings. For example, I'm originally from Scotland, a background that comes with its own set of social cues and expectations. I've had to be mindful of this when working in multicultural settings to ensure that I'm not inadvertently alienating others by relying solely on the context of my own upbringing. Even when working with British and American employees who supposedly speak the "same" language, there are plenty of opportunities for

---

7 (Wargo, 2006)

misunderstanding. I remember working in Europe via Zoom with American colleagues, who suggested "let's table" an item on the agenda. We sat forward expecting to discuss the item. In the UK, to "table" an item is to put it on the table for discussion, while in America, to "table" an item is to shelve it until a later date. Thankfully, much hilarity ensued in this particular case.

However, cultural nuances can create confusion and even frustration if we aren't aware of them. How we interact with others gets even more complex when we add to that the differences in our personalities. On the DiSC personality assessment, as I mentioned, I score as an "ID," meaning I often value bold action. I'm aware that my "Influencer" Style is strongly backed by a high "Dominant" score, which leads to a direct communication style that can unintentionally overwhelm others, especially those with different personality types. These individuals might require more time to process information and contribute their thoughts. Because I know this is how I come across, it is important for me to give others the time they need to contribute. I make an effort not to rush decisions or discussions, allowing space for everyone on the team to participate in a way that's comfortable for them.

A self-aware leader understands their own emotions, strengths, and weaknesses. They recognize that their actions and words have a significant impact on their team. They possess the ability to empathize with others, and this awareness guides them to lead in a way that resonates with and motivates their team. By being in tune with their own emotions and limitations, they foster an environment of trust and open communication, encouraging their team to also embrace self-awareness and authenticity.

To help you best understand how you come across, I recommend using the Johari Window[8] tool. It was developed by psychologists Joseph Luft and Harrington Ingham in 1955, and though it might be an old tool, it is still highly effective and serves to enhance self-awareness and understanding in interpersonal relationships. It also helps you understand both your conscious and unconscious biases.

This tool breaks down your understanding of yourself into four quadrants: what you know you know, what you know you don't know, what you don't know that you know, and what you don't know that you don't know. This exercise can be a bit revealing, and it requires the help of people who know you well. So, I recommend doing it with people who you trust and respect. It is invaluable for identifying blind spots in your behavior or communication style.

The simplest way to go about completing this tool is to:

- Select five adjectives that describe who you are
- Ask a diverse set of people to select five adjectives that describe who you are
- Categorize the results into the four Johari windows
- Discuss the results with the group to elicit deeper insights

I like to think of it as a mirror with four panes, each pane revealing a different aspect of yourself. The first pane reflects what

---

8 (MindTools, n.d.)

you already know about yourself and what others know about you too. This is the "public" you, the part of yourself that is openly acknowledged and understood. The second pane shows what you know about yourself that others don't. This is your "private" self, the part of you that you've chosen to keep hidden from the world. Maybe you come across as highly confident, but you struggle sometimes with imposter syndrome—or maybe you are more of an introvert with more need for quiet downtime than you acknowledge. The third pane reveals what others see in that you don't know about yourself. These are your blind spots. Just like you might miss a smudge of dirt on your face unless someone points it out, there are aspects of your behavior or character that you may be unaware of. The fourth pane is completely dark, symbolizing what neither you nor others know about you. This "unknown" quadrant contains untapped potential, unexplored fears, and skills or characteristics you may not even be aware you have.

It's easy to focus on the flattering reflections—the qualities that make you feel competent and confident. But I believe true growth occurs in the uncomfortable zones, the areas that reveal your blind spots or untapped potential. A willingness to explore these aspects, even when they make you squirm, is required for meaningful self-improvement. You may discover, for example, that you come off as abrasive when you thought you were being direct—or, on the other hand, that you have a knack for inspiring others that you hadn't fully recognized. In a leadership role, understanding how you're perceived can help you adapt your style to better motivate your team, resolve conflicts, and build a more cohesive working environment.

I've seen this firsthand. I worked alongside an exceptional HR director who reported to me and came from the operational side of our dual-headquartered company. Her knack for communication was unique. She knew how to adapt language and tone to resonate with different audiences, from hourly employees to degreed management, whether they came from our urban or rural offices. She could always bridge the communication gap in a conversation, and her ability to read the room and create a welcoming atmosphere inspired me.

She could do this because she was highly self-aware. She knew exactly how she came across and what aspects of her communication she might need to change to better resonate with different audiences. This doesn't mean she was a different person—far from it. She never tried to be anyone other than herself. But she knew how she would come across, and she made sure she continually communicated effectively with everyone in the room.

This blend of self-knowledge and adaptability is what sets apart great leaders. They are not rigid in their methods. They understand their strengths and weaknesses and possess the agility to modify their behavior for the greater good of their team. They never stop evolving.

Establish Your Behavioral Principles

The process of outlining your guiding behavioral principles is integral to understanding and enhancing how you come across as a leader.

Just as laying a strong foundation is essential for the stability and success of a building, establishing clear behavioral expectations is foundational for building a resilient and high-performing team. This process begins with a deep dive into your own leadership style and the values you embody. When you articulate and live by these guiding behavioral principles, you provide a clear model for how challenges should be approached, how interactions should be handled, and what values should drive decision-making. This clarity helps your team understand what is expected of them *and* what they can expect from you.

Think of these principles as the "rules of engagement" for how team members should interact with each other, approach challenges, and represent the organization. When everyone in a team understands and adheres to these principles, it creates a harmonious environment. Everyone knows what is expected of them. Let's be honest, we all do better when we know what values we are expected to embody. There is less ambiguity about expectations, leading to fewer misunderstandings and conflicts.

Leaders should lay out these behavioral guiding principles for individual teams at the onset of any project. I've found that this significantly increases the likelihood of success. According to an article on Indeed, "Guiding principles help managers and their teams create, develop, and maintain company cultures that help businesses grow."[9]

---

9 (Indeed, 2023)

These guiding principles often stem from the core values of the company, which should be the basis for the behavior of every employee, regardless of their team. Yet, it's all too common for organizations to establish these principles only to metaphorically put them on a shelf (or on their website) and never actively use them with intent in day-to-day work life. This is a critical mistake! Core values and guiding principles shouldn't just be a ceremonial aspect of corporate culture; they should actively influence day-to-day operations and decision-making.

It's important to take them off the shelf and integrate them into regular discussions, performance reviews, and especially in one-on-one meetings with direct reports. A current colleague of mine, who was previously the leader of the best place to work in the finance industry (at Pacific Mercantile Bank, in California, one of the largest markets in the world), takes this very seriously. He is now leading the charge to develop a visionary new digital bank based in Arizona, with great success! You can bet he takes the guiding behavioral principles of his teams very seriously, and it reflects in the extraordinary cultures he builds. He was part of a team tasked with the closing of many banks during the 2008 financial crisis, and he frequently reminds us that the banks that closed down failed because of the lack of behavioral principles, poor cultures, and poor leadership.

When creating behavioral guidelines, don't craft them in isolation. Establishing them from an "ivory tower" without the input of the people who will be guided by them is a recipe for failure. I've always found it more effective to include the perspectives of those I manage when shaping goals and strategic plans. Yes, it may take longer, but this approach ensures that everyone is on the same page and invested in the plan from the get-go.

This level of clarity helps to set everyone up for success by eliminating guesswork and ambiguity. It creates an environment where people feel secure in their roles and empowered to make decisions that align with the shared values and principles. The fusion of authentic leadership and clear guiding principles creates a workplace culture where both individual and collective successes are far more attainable.

To establish and implement your behavioral guidelines, follow these steps:

1. **Conduct a Vision and Values Workshop:** Organize a workshop with key stakeholders to align on the company's vision, mission, and collective values. Your behavioral principles should keep these things in mind.

2. **Solicit Input from Team Leaders:** Before finalizing behavioral principles, involve team leaders from different departments. Encourage them to provide input based on their experiences and the unique challenges their teams face.

3. **Draft and Refine:** Based on the feedback received, draft a set of behavioral principles that embody the organization's values. Refine this draft through further discussions until a consensus is reached on principles that are both aspirational and actionable.

4. **Integrate into Daily Activities:** Agree with your team on how these principles will manifest as guidelines for day-to-day activities. This could be as simple as starting meetings with a principle-related reflection or as integrated as a checklist for decision-making processes.

5. **Establish a Feedback Loop:** Build the discussion of these behaviors into daily feedback loops and regular performance reviews. This consistent reinforcement helps to solidify the principles as part of the organizational DNA, encouraging employees to internalize and embody these values-based behaviors in their work.

6. **Recognize and Award:** Consider establishing awards or recognitions for individuals or teams who exemplify these principles exceptionally well. Doing so will reinforce the importance of these behaviors and motivate others to align their actions.

As a leader, your adherence to these behavioral principles is paramount. Demonstrate through your actions how these principles guide your decisions and interactions. Leading by example is the most powerful tool in ensuring these principles are taken seriously throughout the organization.

A word of caution to CEOs: the importance of having the right people in leadership roles who genuinely reflect your organization's behavioral principles cannot be overstated. If there's a misalignment, you will find that meeting your goals—whether they are related to revenue, profitability, customer satisfaction, growth, or employee engagement—becomes an uphill battle. I've seen time and time again leaders who don't embody the values and principles of the company end up stifling progress and eroding the corporate culture.

There aren't any exceptions here. Make leaders who embody your organization's behavioral principles a priority.

I vividly remember being on an eight-person Executive Team leading a global hyper-growth company that had staked out its values based on the principles of transparency, integrity, and respect. Over the previous three years, the executive team had worked cohesively together, and those principles had been clearly and consistently applied throughout the headquarter employee base. Unfortunately, there hadn't been an effort to extend this commitment to behavioral principles to the US Field Leadership, a group of whom had begun to exert their demands and wield authority over their international colleagues as well as the CEO.

The lack of adherence to our much-vaunted principles began to fragment the group, and many of us experienced the horror of helplessly watching as the fabric of the company started to unravel. Groups formed alliances and splintered the previous leadership cohesion. And this division made company goals and values unclear to employees.

The CEO had known that some of the Field Leadership individuals did not ascribe to the company value set and were in fact "poisoning the well," but they had not been ejected due to their high performance. That was a grave mistake. The company is now a fraction of its previous size. Too late, the CEO learned the importance of taking care of culture to ensure longevity.

Bottom line—behavioral principles and guidelines *have* to be intentionally introduced and embraced across all leadership and constantly nurtured to ensure a company's health and sustainability. When the behavioral expectations are clear, so is your leadership style. Your image as a leader will shift to one who is approachable, clear, and deeply committed to fostering an environment where everyone is encouraged to thrive.

Intentionality Is Key

When I worked in the European office of a Global Corporation, overseeing projects across 33 different markets, my work caught the attention of one of the company's founders.

He was putting a new leadership team together and came to visit me in the UK, where he asked if I might have an interest in transferring (with my family) to the US to head up Marketing Programs worldwide. I was thrilled! Once I confirmed my interest, he invited me and my family to take a trip to the US to see if we would be comfortable making the move. Six months later, after much preparation (selling the UK house, applying for visas, relocation, US corporate housing, new schools, finding a new home and furniture and cars), my husband and I found ourselves living in the US as expats with our 9-year-old and 6-year-old daughters.

Admittedly, it was a whirlwind of a change.

As I settled into my new role, I found myself at the helm of expanding existing projects and spearheading new ones. My team now spanned continents, with my UK direct reports continuing under my leadership, complemented by a fresh US team. It was a unique opportunity to meld diverse perspectives into a cohesive unit. Diving headfirst into this challenge, I prioritized crafting a distinct culture for our newly formed department. This meant actively listening to everyone's challenges, celebrating their achievements, and encouraging their input to our future strategies.

It was a big move in every aspect. I think it succeeded due to recognition of and preparedness to embrace an opportunity when it came along and my commitment and conscious intention to stay grounded in what matters throughout.

Throughout your career, you are the primary architect of your own success. You have invested blood, sweat, and tears to reach your current position, and you don't deserve to experience subpar leadership that diminishes your achievements or "punches down" at you when you try hard. Your journey to leadership, whether you are in the C-suite or you are still climbing the ladder, reflects the sum of your past choices, your resilience against negativity, and your unwavering commitment to your principles.

You have to be intentional as you progress. In the same way that you can't rely on others for your happiness, you also can't rely solely on external leadership to guide you towards professional success. Building leadership qualities within yourself—by continually learning, adapting, and growing—ensures that you become the kind of leader you wish to see in the world (thanks, Gandhi). Whether it's mastering the art of communication, developing deeper emotional intelligence, or understanding how to leverage diverse talents, each step you take in improving yourself equips you to be a better leader for others.

If we want our corporate cultures to shift from toxic to empowering, the change starts with learning how to be the leaders we wish we could have experienced.

Fear Is Normal

As leaders, the way we come across to others is key in shaping our team's culture, motivation, and ultimately their success. But what often goes unnoticed is how fear often influences our leadership style and, by extension, our perceived identity in the workplace.

During my tenure in Europe, ahead of my move to the US, I reported to an American boss. The geographical distance inadvertently granted me a higher degree of empowerment than I might have experienced in a more traditional office setting. I adhered to the tasks at hand, diligently working on proposals, formulating plans, securing approvals, and executing projects. But with the physical distance between me and my boss, I had the space to explore new approaches that I believed were necessary and effective for the region and the company.

By listening to the input of the marketing teams across the European markets, I was able to work with them to coalesce our vision, product needs, and marketing strategies into one European proposal. Several of these projects caught the attention, and approval, of the US Headquarter leadership. Having the latitude to step back and consider the bigger picture allowed me more time to paint the picture of what *could be* in a way that inspired others to support. It's amazing what is possible when micromanagement is not present!

Despite the excitement of scaling projects internationally, there was of course always an undercurrent of fear—fear of the unknown, fear of failure, and fear of not living up to expectations. However, if I had let my fears influence my leadership, I would not have made an impact on the company. Moments like this don't happen if you play it safe.

Our fear can distort how we come across to others. It might push us to adopt an overly assertive stance, where we overcompensate for our insecurities by being excessively directive or controlling. Or our fear might manifest as excessive caution, where the dread of making mistakes or facing conflict leads to indecision and a reluctance to take necessary risks.

In both scenarios, the leader's unchecked fear undermines their effectiveness and significantly impacts productivity.

It's important to recognize that fear is a universal experience, especially in leadership roles where the stakes are high. However, it's how we manage and respond to this fear that defines our leadership presence. Do we let it hide our true selves, leading through a facade of confidence while internally grappling with doubt? Or do we acknowledge our fears, viewing them as opportunities for growth and genuine connection with our team?

The latter approach not only humanizes us as leaders, but also enhances our authenticity. When team members see their leader facing fears and vulnerabilities with integrity, it fosters a culture of trust and openness.

The allure of "peacocking," or showcasing your achievements and talents, may seem like a fast track to garnering respect. It might even get you promoted faster if you are really good at managing up. However, this only serves to fuel ego-centric behaviors and will alienate team members by making them feel less competent or valued. In Susan Jeffers book, *Feel the Fear and Do It Anyway*[10], she says, "Remember that underlying all our fears is a lack of trust in ourselves." We fear failure, and we fear judgment. We hope the mask we put on will allow us to be whoever or whatever we need to be to avoid all the things we fear.

According to Stefan Falk, an executive coach and workplace psychology expert, feeling insecure is a natural human experience. However, Falk, known for his work in "Intrinsic Motivation: Learn to Love Your Work and Succeed as Never Before" and as a co-author of Neuroleadership, points out a critical issue. He explains, "While feeling insecure is natural, problematic behaviors can develop when people consistently attempt to conceal or compensate for their self-doubt."[11]

---

10 (Jeffers, 2006)
11 (Falk, 2023)

Remember this when you feel pressured to adhere to traditional leadership models. The security offered by "playing it safe" is often illusory. Think about leaders you admire in your life. More often than not, you will find their paths to success involve a crucial moment of bold, fear-filled decision-making that forces them to step beyond the familiar confines of their comfort zone. They took a chance; at some point they had to be bold. And that moment likely had a big impact on the leader they are today.

So, I say again—embrace your fears and don't settle for being mediocre.

Chapter Wrap Up

To establish a clear picture of who you are so others can better understand you, you should:

- Use a tool such as the Johari Window to better understand how you come across so you can mitigate your blind spots.
- Outline your behavioral principles to provide clarity to your team.
- Be intentional about showing your authentic self to those you lead, even if it doesn't come easily.
- If you aren't careful, fear can distort how you come across to others. Don't let it.

Chapter 4:

Set Your Boundaries

Have you clearly established your boundaries? In a broad sense, boundaries are guidelines, rules, or limits that a person creates to identify reasonable, safe, and permissible ways for others to behave towards them. Boundaries also determine how an individual will respond when someone steps outside those limits. They are crucial in establishing one's identity and are an essential part of establishing and maintaining healthy relationships, both personally and professionally.

I firmly believe boundaries are a key aspect of evolved leadership. Good leaders use boundaries to clarify expectations and communicate effectively. The goal is clarity—for both yourself and those you work with. You know where you stand, and others know it too. Setting your boundaries ahead of time means you are prepared and can draw a line in the sand when necessary.

Forbes published an article about how boundaries affect the interactions between leadership and those they manage. They said, "When you have no boundaries, it leaves the other person guessing what the guardrails are in their relationship or interactions with you . . ."[12] And in that same article, they went on to say, "In the workplace, leaders need to set an example for others to follow when it comes to setting and enforcing boundaries."[13]

Setting and being crystal clear with my boundaries has benefitted my career numerous times. One of the positions I took in my career was as the CMO of a relatively new company. They had successfully reached $175 million in revenue on their own, but they had ambitions to grow to half a billion or more in revenue. Which is why they brought me in, since my experience had been in larger organizations. During my three years with them, we grew to over $700 million in revenue.

But that path was far from smooth. During those three years, I established new systems, hired new talent, and implemented new processes. All of which are monumental tasks filled with their own challenges. The biggest challenge of all was the clear resentment from the VP of Marketing, a direct report of mine. She was a powerhouse of a woman who, like me, had been a senior executive at very large Fortune 500 companies. She was also one of the original few who started with the company and often wore countless hats as it grew. Her skills were undeniably extensive and valuable, but when it came time to hire a CMO, the company's leadership brought me in instead of promoting her to the position.

She made it clear that she was furious about it.

---

12 & 13   (Lofgren, 2021)

She was cold, rolled her eyes when I spoke to her, and would gossip about me in hushed whispers. She did everything she could to make sure I didn't feel welcome. I could have taken this personally. It's easy to. Especially when someone is expected to "get with the program" but they refuse to fall in line. This type of insubordination often makes leaders feel like they have some kind of right to press hard on these individuals and force compliance. But rather than take it personally, I chose to see beyond the surface.

I realized that her frustration wasn't so much with me but with the situation. Here was a talented individual who had given her all to the company, only to get passed up when the chance for a promotion came her way. How would you feel in that situation? Even if you aren't the best person for the job, anger is the typical response from anyone in the same situation. But using empathy and inclusion in my interactions was an internal boundary I wasn't willing to compromise.

So, empathy became my tool of choice. Her talent was undeniable, and I wanted her to be part of my team. She had a history of the company I didn't and a deep brand management and marketing skill set. So I communicated openly with her, seeking her opinions, acknowledging her contributions, and sharing my vision. I never tried to get her to like me. And I wasn't trying to placate or pacify her. Instead, my goal was to genuinely recognize her worth regardless of how she might feel about me.

As I learned more about her, I found she had a difficult childhood where her ambitions had never been supported, and she was consistently faced with having to go above and beyond to prove her worth, fighting against toxicity throughout her life and her career. Due to much of this experience, she had developed a bit of a brittle exterior, and she had some understandable resentment. In truth, she had a real chip on her shoulder for business leaders in general. But I stuck to my guns anyway because I could see why she was mad, I could understand her position of hurt and defensiveness, and I could see her strength and huge potential.

As time wore on, the icy walls melted. Our professional relationship blossomed, rooted in trust and mutual respect, and we became the team we needed to be to help the company succeed. Even after we moved on from that company, we continued to collaborate for years and still do to this day. Now, she runs her own company and was recently asked to go to a major university to give a speech on leadership. She gave a marvelous talk on the topic of lessons in life and leadership. There was even a moment in the speech where she talked about our relationship and the positive impact we have had on each other!

Holding my boundary of empathy and inclusion and responding to her situation with respect instead of anger made this situation (which, let's be honest, could have ended badly) into a positive for us and the company. Instead of demanding respect from her, I nurtured our working relationship, and we went on to create a partnership which benefitted us both for years to come.

Facing every situation and person I meet with empathy and inclusion is a boundary for me. And it has become a north star for how I interact with the world. When times are hard, it has guided me to make choices that are authentic to me and my values.

You need to choose your boundaries and treat them like your north star. Even when things get hard. Doing so will help you become a more consistent leader and allow you to navigate complex situations with a clear idea of how you should handle them. If you haven't thought about what your boundaries should be, and difficult situations arise, you'll find yourself reacting based on your emotions, instead of reacting based on your values. And that is where we often make regrettable mistakes that could affect our image and our careers.

Set Your *Internal* Boundaries

There is a noticeable difference in the way many leaders conduct themselves in professional environments versus their personal life. It's like switching on a light. The moment they walk through the office doors, they switch to a professional persona, which is part of the mask we discussed in chapter two.

Exhausting, right? I know I can't thrive when I'm constantly trying to be something different than what I am. I've always believed that authenticity beats rehearsed perfection. Every. Single. Time. Why? Because realness is relatable. It's why I never wore a mask at work. I didn't want to be unapproachable, and I never wanted to be an enigma for my direct reports. Instead, I wanted them to see me as a real person who was on their side and to know I would approach situations with empathy, fairness, and curiosity.

When you consciously choose to act in a certain way and have clearly established boundaries, you set the tone for those around you. They understand what to expect from you and know they won't be surprised. They feel more comfortable sharing ideas, questions, and concerns with you.

If a direct report thinks they will be punished or looked down on if they do anything but agree with you, you are doing something wrong. There are plenty of folks who will nod along with their boss's every word, not necessarily out of respect or agreement, but mainly because . . . well, they are the boss. This inherent hierarchy can be our downfall in leadership because the way we act will be reflected in our team. It's always nice to have agreement and alignment. But if that agreement is out of sheer deference rather than genuine understanding, you are building your leadership on shaky grounds.

Inconsistency isn't leadership, it is performance. And people can see right through it. Setting internal boundaries for yourself will help you break away from this dance.

Internal boundaries are guidelines we set for ourselves relating to our thoughts, emotions, values, and attitudes. Unlike external boundaries, which have to do with the limits you set with other people, these internal boundaries are aligned with our personal values. They reflect your integrity and are the guardrails we need to become our best selves. Sticking to these boundaries consistently is what sets apart evolved and exceptional leaders from those leaders who add to our stress.

When you don't have these internal boundaries established, it's easy to be swayed by high stress situations or to treat people differently based on their status or what they can offer you. This lack of internal discipline often leads to inconsistent behavior, where your actions are influenced more by external pressures than by your core principles. True respect and trust are earned when people see you treat everyone with the same level of kindness, fairness, and respect, regardless of the situation. This consistency, fostered by your internal boundaries, becomes your signature, your *personal brand* that people come to know you by.

When deciding these internal boundaries that help define how you treat others, ask yourself:

What behaviors towards others make me feel proud and authentic?

When have I felt my integrity compromised by how I've treated someone, and what would I do differently?

What actions from others have made me feel disrespected or undervalued, and how can I ensure I don't replicate them?

How do I want to be remembered by those I interact with, and what treatment aligns with that legacy?

What are the absolute "no-go" zones in how I react and respond to others, even in challenging situations?

When your internal boundaries are clear and deeply rooted in your values, they act as a natural filter, warding off behaviors that don't serve you or your organization and welcoming those that do. In doing so, you create a culture of integrity around you, leading by example and encouraging others to follow suit.

Set Your *External* Boundaries

External boundaries are the limits you set with other people. They govern how others can behave around you and how you respond to their behavior. These boundaries are about protecting your space, energy, and well-being from external forces, and not about controlling other people. They allow you to communicate your needs and expectations clearly, avoid being taken advantage of, and maintain respect and dignity in your interactions with others.

Our external boundaries are just as important as our internal boundaries. Your team will likely *see* your external boundaries and *feel* your internal boundaries. However, the two work together to establish your leadership style.

Often setting external leadership boundaries means:

1. Nixing the gossip. You don't indulge in it, and you sure as hell don't entertain it.
2. Giving honest, constructive feedback. Overlooking issues doesn't make them disappear.
3. Staying true to your word. No lying. No cheating. No shortcuts.
4. Not stepping on someone else to climb that corporate ladder. There's plenty of room at the top for good performers.
5. Rejecting backdoor dealings. No conspiring to outmaneuver colleagues or working against the company's interests.

The main question to ask yourself when setting an external boundary is whether the conversation you are taking part in, or observing, would be just as comfortable in front of a wider audience? Asking yourself this question pushes you to consider the transparency and appropriateness of your interactions. If the answer to that question is no, you likely need an external boundary on the action or topic.

Sometimes, setting these external boundaries can feel confrontational. Trust me, I've been there. But strong leaders can't go around avoiding ruffling feathers. It's easy to be tempted to forgo these boundaries, especially behind closed doors or when the going gets tough. And there will be moments when bending these principles might seem like the quickest or easiest route to success. But remember, every choice you make isn't just about you; it's a ripple effect on your team and the entire company.

Don't settle for mediocrity. It's not worth it! Even when it is easier to gloss over feedback that should be given, or situations where you would rather give a vague statement to avoid discomfort rather than address an elephant in the room. Sometimes it's even easier to let gossip continue because you want to be popular and accepted among your peers. But if you do this, someone will always lose—both the people gossiping, and the person being gossiped about. You need to be a better version of yourself that will enable others around you to be better versions of themselves.

Never settling isn't just about the big moments, though they are important. It's also about the micro-behaviors—the small choices we make daily. It's in the nuances, the in-between moments, where true leadership is often tested. When you come to these crossroads in your career with knowledge of what you will accept, and what you won't, you will have a clear path forward.

External Leadership Boundaries You Can Adopt

Your external leadership boundaries should be in line with your values and guiding behavioral principles. But here are a few green flag boundaries I used that you might like to adopt:

1. Punctuality as a Form of Respect
   - Meetings start on time. If a meeting is scheduled for 9:00, start then.
   - In case of unavoidable delays, ensure everyone is informed ahead of time.
   - Request rescheduling only if absolutely essential and pivotal to the meeting's purpose.

2. Respecting the Tone of Communication
   - Be clear about acceptable language. For example, if swearing isn't appropriate in a particular setting, communicate it. Note that constructive criticism is welcome, and complaining is not. Describe the difference.
   - If gossip arises, firmly explain why the conversation is inappropriate to prevent fostering a toxic environment.

3. Addressing Toxicity Proactively
- Immediate action is essential when someone is creating a hostile environment.
- Remember: It's better to nurture a C-player with a good culture fit than to tolerate a toxic A-player. Every extra day a toxic player continues to be allowed to remain, more poison is seeping into the corporate culture.

4. Honor Your Commitments
- Be consistent in keeping your promises.
- Establish trust by ensuring your actions align with your words.

5. Open-Door Policy & Structured Time
- Designate specific times when your door is open for team members to approach you.
- Use the rest of your time efficiently for strategizing and attending meetings.

6. Feedback Is a Two-Way Street
- Implement skip-level feedback meetings to monitor and enhance team dynamics. A trusting, transparent culture doesn't just happen because you wish for it. You must be intentional and committed to making it so.
- Keep communication channels open to ensure everyone is aligned and informed.

7. Preventing the Blame Game
- If issues arise, bring all involved parties together for a transparent discussion. Doing so will discourage finger-

pointing if those complaining know all parties will address the issue together.

As a final note on setting your external leadership boundaries, remember that *your* boundary should never be about controlling someone else. The University of Guelph published an article on Boundaries vs. Controlling Behaviors and the differences between them. They said, "A boundary is something we might set, not as a way to control others, but to express what we're willing and unwilling to engage with. The goal of boundaries is to create limits around what safety, relationships, and interactions look like for us. Control is meant to make others do what you want them to do."[14]

Reflect on the intentions behind your boundaries. Are they genuinely set to protect your well-being, the well-being of others, and foster mutual respect? Or are they veiled attempts at manipulation and power play? The best boundaries are those that are clear, rooted in self-awareness, and come from a place of genuine care. It's a delicate balance but one that's needed for genuine, constructive connections.

Without Boundaries, We Can Lose Ourselves

As a leader, you are always being watched.

Not in a creepy way (don't worry, no one is outside your window), but as an example. Anytime a question is asked, a situation arises, or direction is needed, people will watch and wait

---

14 (Unknown, 2023)

for your reaction. Then they will follow your lead. Every choice, every action, becomes an example for those around you.

I know that might feel like a heavy weight on your shoulders, but it is the price of leadership.

This constant visibility is why setting and adhering to clear boundaries is vital. Without them, it's all too easy to lose focus, to drift into the gray areas where principles can become compromised and leadership diluted. Your boundaries are the framework within which you operate. They keep you grounded, even when the pressure mounts. They are the safeguards that ensure you act with consistency. They are the silent, yet powerful communicators of what is valued and what is not. By holding firm to your limits, you teach others to respect them, and in turn, to set and honor their own.

In the minutiae of everyday decisions, you demonstrate your leadership philosophy in the way you address a conflict, give feedback, or credit a colleague. It is in these moments that you have the opportunity to cement your reputation as a leader. If you take someone else's lead in terms of behavioral principles—which might include talking behind someone's back, swearing, not turning up on time, or not keeping your word—it can ruin your integrity. And the loss of integrity is, in essence, the loss of one's reputation.

When Someone Breaks Your Boundaries

I wish I could tell you everything will be smooth sailing, and no one will break your boundaries, but unfortunately, people will likely push against them at some point in your career.

I knew a young millennial woman who led communications for a renowned brand. Although praised by the leadership for her ability, internally she was overwhelmed. The higher-ups were indecisive, their decisions ever-changing, and they piled on responsibilities without clear direction. She was quickly pushed to her limits, and she decided to set a boundary.

Instead of juggling the influx of tasks as they came in, she would say, "I've received your request. Can you clarify your priorities?"

She was constructive and polite in her approach, acknowledged the work coming her way, then asked for clarity of priority because she could not get to everything all at once. For weeks, nothing much changed. The various leaders (including her actual boss) sent an enormous number of requests her way and verbally acknowledged the mountainous workload, but they didn't change their behavior, and the demand level consequently continued unabated. I counseled her to maintain her professionalism, but to continue to repeat the need for prioritization "like a broken record."

When those above us are pushing us to do more, conversations like this are daunting. And when we see someone breaking a boundary, it can be hard to call them out on it. However, she followed my advice, and bit by bit, the work requests became more streamlined and prioritized. Now discussions are underway to provide the necessary direct reports to support this hard-working professional and A-player.

This challenge had a good outcome for two reasons. The employee stuck to her guns regarding the boundary she had set, *and* she remained professional in her approach. Which is difficult to do, especially when you feel like you are drowning.

I bet you can think of a time when your boundaries were clearly broken. When someone stepped over the line, leaving you feeling disrespected. Maybe they pushed you to do something you didn't want to do. Maybe they tried to get you to take part in gossip you wanted to stay away from. Do you remember what that experience was like? Do you remember how it made you feel? The discomfort that comes in these situations is from stepping out of alignment with ourselves. Some of us are good about speaking up when this happens. But many others let resentment build instead of speaking out.

We cannot ignore these problems because they only grow. You have to speak up and let others know when they have crossed the line. If you are a leader, this is even more important to address immediately.

Here are six actions you can take when your boundaries are violated:

1. Initiate the Difficult Dialogue

Begin with a candid, human-to-human conversation. It's possible the other person is blissfully unaware of how their actions or words affect you. Try starting the conversation with, "I've noticed that when you do/say [specific action or words], it comes across as [how it makes you feel]. Is that what you intended?" By framing it this way, you are seeking to understand instead of making accusations.

2. Make the Invisible Visible

Many people, unfortunately, lack self-awareness. By illuminating the impact of their behavior, you might be giving them an opportunity for growth and self-improvement. Most people genuinely don't want to hurt you, and to hear that they did, said in a kind and respectful way, will give them an opportunity to address the issue and help them grow.

3. Embrace the Discomfort

Navigating tough conversations can be, well, uncomfortable. But avoiding them? That can have long-term repercussions on your reputation, well-being, and professional relationships. Make it a point to lean into the discomfort; it's where growth happens.

4. Stay Firm in Your Convictions

Once you've set a boundary, commit to it. This might mean practicing how you'll respond if someone crosses that line again or seeking support from trusted colleagues or mentors. This time is well spent. That way, when you have to speak up, you already know exactly what you will say.

5. Seek Higher Assistance

If direct conversations aren't working, it may be time to involve HR. But tread with caution here. Not every HR department prioritizes employee well-being over company interests. Instead of going on the defensive, approach HR with the goal of finding a solution. You can say something like, "I've been facing this issue and tried resolving it through conversation. I'd appreciate any guidance or help in addressing it further."

6. Collaborate with Leadership

Don't forget your immediate supervisor or manager. They are in a position to mediate, advise, or even put an end to boundary violations. Share your concerns and work together to find a resolution. Using the same dialogue as I mentioned in #5 can help here.

Your boundaries reflect your values, self-respect, and professional integrity. Standing up for them paves the way for a more respectful and harmonious workplace for everyone. Unfortunately, there may be times when all the above simply don't solve the problem. If you find yourself in a workplace which constantly disrespects your boundaries, and none of the above has worked to resolve it, it may be time to move on. There are days we all wake up, reluctant to face the office. But if these days turn into weeks and months, and your spirit feels crushed, get out as soon as you can.

This isn't to say that every challenging phase should have you heading for the exit. Every role, every company, will have its highs and lows. If there's growth, both personal and professional, and a salary that mirrors your effort, perhaps there's more to gain. But if you feel you are no longer earning, learning, and growing in a role, it is no longer for you.

Staying too long in a noxious environment is like standing in quicksand and hoping you'll stop sinking instead of actively pulling yourself out—and the longer you are in these situations, the harder it becomes to leave. These environments can cloud judgment, erode confidence, and make brighter horizons seem unreachable. Sometimes, for your own sanity and well-being, it's essential to wrench yourself from a place before it drowns your spirit. Ideally, the company will intervene on your behalf. But if an organization can't see beyond a toxic manager or fails to prioritize employee well-being, then perhaps their priorities don't align with your own.

Many companies have lost individuals because their environment, or even one specific leader, was toxic. I know several professionals who have loved their job but had one leader who consistently mistreated them. Many of these people tried to reach out to the individual directly to solve the problem and even lodged formal complaints. But no change happened, and they were stuck in a toxic situation.

Do not tolerate this. A company that fails to address issues of toxicity within the culture is no place to be. No individual, regardless of their rank or performance, should be allowed to poison the well. In the end, what's the use of a high performer if their toxicity drives away the collective talent of an organization?

Dig Deep and Find Courage

After parting ways with a company under a mutual agreement, I ventured into a project with a couple of friends focused on women's empowerment. This initiative was all about uplifting and building a community of supportive women. It had nothing in common with my previous employer's business model. Theirs was a consumer products company; ours was a community platform—what you might call a "passion project" of giving back.

Yet, they slapped us with a cease and desist, falsely accusing us of competition.

My partners and I weren't going to let this slide. We knew we weren't in the wrong. So, we fought back. We wrote to the CEO, clarifying the misunderstanding, but found ourselves nevertheless entangled in a lengthy legal battle. The odds seemed stacked against us. We had a small legal team, while the company hired one of the city's biggest law firms. If we lost, the financial consequences would be enormous. Not only would we not recover the money owed to us, but we would also have to cover the legal costs of both parties.

Despite all these risks, we stood our ground and won the case!

There were many times during that process when I knew it would have been easier to back down. But sometimes, you have to face your Goliath. It's not an easy path but standing up to them is 100x better than being pushed around and defeated by toxic people and letting them smother your spirit.

When you let unacceptable things slide, you are compromising your boundaries. On a less dramatic but potentially more insidious note, if, in your day-to-day life, you see something that should not have happened, the easy route—ignore it, pretend you didn't notice, or rationalize it as a one-time thing—is tempting.

After all, it might seem insignificant in the moment. But silence can, unknowingly, become complicity. And over time, what you ignore, or overlook may grow and threaten to distort your values and contribute to you losing your way.

The title of "leader" or "boss" carries with it the responsibility to call out behaviors that create toxicity. These moments demand courage. They challenge you to be brave and take a stand. Not just for your own well-being, but for the larger good of the organization and its collective conscience. Digging deep and finding the courage to do something about a crossed boundary can be difficult. We tend to underreact or overreact because we are emotionally charged and can't think straight. But we can't let these moments pass by unaddressed.

Even when addressing what happened is harder than letting it go.

There is no teacher or parent to shield you from unfair treatment. Even your boss might not always be the protector you need. The stark reality is that you are your own defender.

Too often, I've seen dedicated individuals pour their heart into their jobs, striving to be better every day. Yet, they falter when it comes to defending themselves against unfair treatment. I fully believe standing up for yourself is a necessity. You need to believe in the boundaries you set and believe that you are worth fighting for. Your worth, your dignity, and your well-being depend on it.

Chapter Wrap Up

When setting your boundaries, remember:

- Internal boundaries are your north star for how you treat others.

- External boundaries help you define what you will and won't accept from others, but they are not a way to control those around us.

- Without understanding your internal and external boundaries beforehand, you could lose focus when difficult situations arise.

- When someone breaks your boundaries, speak up and follow the steps outlined above, so that you'll be able to handle these problems with grace.

- When you let unacceptable things slide, you are compromising your values and letting yourself down.

Chapter 5:

Embrace Servant Leadership

Authoritative leadership is a one-way street—commands flow downhill, and employees execute. But servant leadership is a two-way conversation. It's collaborative, it requires emotional intelligence, and it focuses on empowering the team. In this model of leadership, those in charge strive to be more self-aware, more supportive, and ultimately, more effective.

Think about the different times you have experienced a leader in your life. Did you perform at a high level with a leader who sat in their office handing out orders? Or did you perform better with a leader who stood beside you and rolled up their sleeves asking, "What do you need from me?"

Matt Tenney, the author of *Serve to Be Great*[15] wrote an article in Business Leadership Today about the impact of servant leaders. He said, "Servant leaders provide a great deal of support to team members that helps them cut down on work stress and remove obstacles to doing great work, making it much easier for them to meet and even exceed performance expectations without doing

---

15 (Tenney, Serve to Be Great, 2014)

harm to their mental and physical well-being."[16] When we are backed by someone who is in our corner, we perform better than we ever will when orders are barked at us.

A servant leader is in the game *with* you. Their priority is to ensure you have got everything you need to win. One cannot become a servant leader without a solid sense of self-awareness, intertwined with a generous dose of humility and humanity. Servant leaders don't grandstand or build a personal empire; they serve the team and by extension the company.

Embracing this type of leadership is tricky. Especially when more traditional forms of leadership are the default in the corporate world. However, it *is* possible. And it starts by listening.

When I step into any new role, my first 60-90 days are dedicated to what I call the "listening phase." I am not the first one to speak up in meetings. I do not act like I know everything. I ask questions. I gather an understanding of what has been tried and what hasn't. And I do this because I truly believe that you cannot lead effectively if you don't fully grasp the context your team is working within, the challenges your team faces, or the resources they need to achieve their goals. As part of the executive team, I am always privy to the goals of the company, but understanding the intricacies involved in reaching them is a whole different ball game.

In the listening phase, I tune into the heartbeat of the team. I learn where their strengths lie, what they've attempted in the past, their depth of knowledge and available resources, and the

---

16 (Tenney, Business Leadership Today, n.d.)

hurdles they have encountered previously. I did this before the term "Servant Leader" was coined, but becoming a servant leader is truly the best way to describe how I interact with my teams. By following the servant leadership principles (which we discuss in this chapter), you *too* can become the leader your team actually needs you to be.

Once you've listened and truly immersed yourself in the company's DNA, you are in a much better position to devise a plan that reflects the input of the team. This is the integral part of standing next to your team and rolling up your sleeves that many leaders forget to engage in. With a plan that reflects input from your team, you create a sense of shared ownership and buy-in because they know you have listened to their insights and ideas *before* you have established objectives and goals.

Peter Nulty from Fortune Magazine said, "Of all the skills of leadership, listening is the most valuable—and one of the least understood. Most captains of industry listen only sometimes, and they remain ordinary leaders. But a few, the great ones, never stop listening. That's how they get word before anyone else of unseen problems and opportunities."[17] And a study conducted by Salesforce where they surveyed over 1,500 employees found that someone who feels heard is actually 4.5x more likely to perform at their highest ability[18].

Listening is one of the biggest ways you can show your authenticity. It's a subtle message to the room that you know

17 (Half, 2023)
18 (Salesforce, n.d.)

you don't have all the context others might have, but you are willing to listen first before you implement any changes. When a leader listens first, those who might have initially been skeptical or uncomfortable with a plan you present will begin to see the value in it. They know you have listened, taken their context into consideration, and have been transparent in your research, planning, and iteration. This level of engagement and understanding turns even the most uncertain team members into willing participants in the journey ahead.

Servant Leadership = Authentic Leadership

When each of us were babies, we loved others without judgment. We didn't think we were greater than anyone, we were unburdened by societal expectations, and we were free from the weight of ego. Back then, love and equality were inherent to our being, and any thoughts of superiority did not exist.

As we grew, the world around us started sculpting our perceptions and behaviors. It shaped us into the person we are today with judgment and perceptions that might not be entirely true. Our experiences, the lessons we learned, the cultural and societal norms we absorbed all contribute to the way we perceive the world. And these experiences also often build up the masks we eventually wear. But these masks, shaped by external expectations and pressures and not by our values, can disconnect us from our authentic selves.

Think about it. When you speak to a CEO you want to impress, versus the pizza delivery guy, do you speak differently? If not, I'm impressed! But the vast majority of us will change our tone and the way we act simply because society has taught us expected behaviors for all kinds of individuals. These expected behaviors have taught us that when speaking to the CEO, we should choose our words carefully and present the best version of ourselves. But when speaking to the pizza delivery person, our demeanor might shift to a more casual, less measured conversation. These adjustments in our behavior, often subconscious, are a testament to the roles and expectations society ingrains in us.

The contrast between how we interact with a CEO and the pizza delivery person is reflective of deeper, ingrained societal structures and hierarchies. It's a product of learned behaviors that dictate a certain reverence for authority and status, while inadvertently downplaying the significance of human connection in seemingly mundane interactions. Servant leadership requires us to consciously dismantle these ingrained behaviors. Why? Because they can create barriers to connecting with others on a genuine, human level—barriers that prevent us from leading with empathy and understanding.

By questioning these automatic responses and societal teachings, we can begin to peel back the layers of conditioned behavior. Especially when this conditioned behavior might include stereotypes that make us less effective leaders. To step into the role of a servant leader, you need to deliberately and consciously tune out the leadership stereotypes and expectations imposed by others.

Knowing yourself is key to this process as we discussed previously, but so is trusting yourself. Your inner voice, when listened to closely, can guide you to lead in a way that aligns with your core values and beliefs. Reconnecting with your true self helps you discard judgments and pretenses, enabling you to lead authentically as a servant leader in a way that feels right and uplifts others.

We can do this by:

1. Practicing active listening and empathy
2. Embracing a mindset of continuous personal growth
3. Not relying on external validation to appreciate your self-worth
4. Communicating honestly and with respect
5. Examining actions you don't like and asking yourself why they bother you

Tuning into these insights will help you reconnect with your values and shed any masks you might be using. Only when you are in tune with who you really are and trust that inner voice can you effectively serve your team.

7 Principles of Servant Leadership

Through my career, as I have mentored other leaders, I found there are seven key principles to becoming a servant leader: humanity, humility, integrity, openness, empowerment, engagement, and inclusion.

Let's dive into each.

1. Humanity

Remember, as we mentioned above, we aren't born to judge others or to see the world through a negative lens. But our experiences hard-wire these perceptions into us. If you are going to be a leader of other human beings, you need to be very aware of the difference between perceptions and the truth. We need to strip judgmental behavior away and revert to the open lens we saw others through as a child. Within a company, working with our teams, we have a responsibility to be consciously aware of the context we are creating and to be intentional about making the culture as healthy as possible.

2. Humility

Often misunderstood as a sign of weakness, humility is actually a sign of strength. Humble leaders are confident enough to be transparent and vulnerable and are consequently approachable and relatable. They create a space where open communication and honesty flourish, and they understand the power of admitting mistakes and learning from them. Which, in turn, encourages their team to adopt a similar mindset. This openness to learning and self-improvement enhances personal growth and drives collective progress within the organization.

3. Integrity

Integrity is your ability to act in alignment with your values, regardless of the audience. And let me tell you, when you start really listening to that gut voice of yours, it's powerful! Consciously acting with integrity becomes a source of fulfillment that you achieve from within—no need to depend on an external source.

4. Openness

Remember the Johari Window? You don't know what you don't know. If you don't remain open or assess your blind spots, you could miss out on the best idea in the room or in the company. This is where listening comes in. Openness in leadership sets the tone for the entire team. It's contagious. When you exhibit a willingness to explore, to question, and to listen, you create an environment where your team feels encouraged to do the same.

5. Empowerment

This is where you roll up your sleeves and stand alongside your team, offering what they need to find success. Make sure you make the effort to understand the context, provide the necessary support to all members of the team, and provide the resources to do the job. Then you don't need to look over their shoulders. If you empower them to get the job done, they will get it done well, and much better than they would have done without that knowledge or support. This frees you up to think strategically.

6. Engagement

True engagement in servant leadership is about involving others. It's recognizing and nurturing the potential in each team member as well as giving them the tools, resources, confidence, and permission they need to excel. When leaders invest in their team's growth, the whole organization rises. It's heartbreaking to see bright, capable individuals just punching the clock because they have become disengaged due to poor leadership. Their confidence dwindles, their enthusiasm fades, and their contributions are just a shadow of what they could be. As leaders, we can't just stand by and watch this happen. We've got to ignite that fire, rekindle that passion, and bring back the spirit that helps our teams become fulfilled and thriving individuals.

7. Inclusion

This is a big one for me. Win-win is a powerful concept. If you commit to a win-win outcome, you are saying to any collaborator or colleague that you want to win and you want them to win too. It's strong positioning because you are also saying that you do *not* want either of you to lose. This translates to trust-based collaboration which opens the floodgates to new ideas and new strategies. Some of the best ideas will likely come from including others in the planning process.

My hope is that these seven principles help create a blueprint for you. Each one of them have served me well throughout my career and have helped the teams I managed to enjoy and be inspired by my leadership. All of us want to be the leader others appreciate and talk about. But it's hard work getting there. It takes commitment, and you will make mistakes. This blueprint will help!

When Mistakes Happen, Correct with Love

When leaders transition from traditional leadership to servant leadership, they often worry about the potential mistakes their team will make. After all, they have been taught that micromanaging a team is how to meet deadlines and ensure work gets done correctly. Right? If they stop doing that, won't everything go wrong?

The answer is both yes and no.

Being a servant leader is about making sure everyone has the resources and knowledge they need to be as successful as possible, then getting out of their way. As a servant leader, you need to believe that people come to work to do the right thing. They don't want to make mistakes. They don't want to fail. They want to do a good job.

Servant leadership is rooted in the belief that most people are inherently motivated and eager to do well, especially when they start a new job full of excitement and ambition. They arrive with enthusiasm, ready to contribute and make a difference. This perspective means when someone's performance falters, we don't jump to conclusions or default to blame. Instead, we dig deeper. We ask questions about their resources, their readiness and fit for the specific role, their personal circumstances, and whether they have the necessary support and coaching.

This approach often reveals performance issues are not about a lack of desire to do well but about obstacles that need to be addressed. And it's where the real responsibility of a leader comes into play: *candid, constructive feedback and guidance given with clarity.*

When someone makes a mistake, find out what went wrong and ask questions. Make it part of your internal boundaries to be curious and non-judgmental about mistakes. Assuming the worst will never help the situation. Cynicism leads to micromanagement, power plays, and dictatorial behaviors—the very antithesis of what servant leadership stands for.

If you believe someone wants to do the best job they can, even when they have failed, you are much more likely to come up with ways to help them perform better. If the guidance you provide doesn't work, they likely don't have the skills they need for the job. In this case, you have the opportunity to help them understand what their strengths are and help outplace them to somewhere that can use their talents.

I had the privilege of attending a number of excellent leadership training courses through GE. One of many memorable lessons that resonated with me occurred when one of the trainers challenged us to think about an unfortunately common occurrence. He described a 55-year-old in an executive role—with a big mortgage and kids in college—who lost their position. They had been climbing the corporate ladder, but every step of the way, their direct boss did not have the courage to provide the candid, constructive feedback that was necessary for their development. They didn't know what they didn't know until it was too late!

Now, because their leaders had never helped them understand when and how they weren't performing well, they lost their position. Wouldn't you feel blindsided in that moment?

Nobody should be surprised they are being let go. Leaders who don't give candid and constructive feedback with clarity are only hurting those they work with. They are not doing anyone any favors by remaining in their comfort zone and failing to provide pointers that could shape someone's career path in a successful direction.

People deserve a chance to correct their mistakes or find a better fit. In an ideal situation, effective leadership would have identified the mismatch in skills and industry fit much earlier in this 55-year-old's career. An insightful leader, practicing servant leadership, would have recognized their struggle. And instead of letting them struggle or advance mistakenly, the leader would have had a candid conversation with them, pointing out where their true strengths lie and how they might better align with another industry or profession.

These conversations aren't easy. It is a huge responsibility to give open and honest feedback. But if you assume most people want to do a good job, you will find ways to help them find a better fit—within your organization or outside of it—earlier in their career. Starting with a simple "Tell me what your thinking was when you did X" is a great way to open the discussion.

Creating a safe space starts with the leader's reaction to mistakes. Remember, as we mentioned before, everyone is watching you as a leader. By approaching these situations with curiosity and an open mind, you set the tone for the culture moving forward.

Self-Governance Is Required

Have you ever "flown off the handle"?

Maybe a stressful project went really wrong or someone rear-ended you when you were already having a bad day. In those moments, we can go from simmering with frustration to boiling over with anger. We shout, we embarrass ourselves, and we usually regret our outburst immediately.

Self-governance is the ability to regulate one's own emotions, thoughts, and behaviors in a disciplined and balanced way. It involves taking personal responsibility for one's actions and reactions, rather than being driven by external pressures or fleeting emotions. For some of us, this is difficult. Especially if we grew up in homes where reacting with emotion instead of logic is the norm.

But, once we reconnect with ourselves and act with authenticity and intentionality, self-governance becomes easier.

Think about the leaders in your life who are quick to anger. One thing goes wrong, and BOOM—their entire day is ruined, and now yours is too, because they make whatever is angering them your problem. We have all experienced leaders we need to tip-toe around on hard days or challenging projects. They raise our blood pressure, make us stressed, and do nothing to aid the morale of a team.

If you take anything away from this book, let it be this: do **not** be this leader.

Make it a point to reconnect with yourself because the shift towards authentic action propels us from simply reacting to external challenges to actively deciding how we react based on our core values, principles, and guiding behaviors. When you consistently align your actions with your core values, you cultivate trust and credibility within your team in a palpable and powerful way.

I'm not saying this is always easy. It is challenging when a thousand things come your way, all of them are high priority, and half of them are already fires by the time they get to your desk. Self-governance is a continual process; some days you will do it well, and other days you will slip. You are only human, after all, but reflecting on those moments when you did slip will help you establish how to govern yourself in the future.

Here are a few questions to help:

- Do my daily actions reflect my core values?
- How do I respond to setbacks, and do I recommit to my goals afterward?
- Am I consistent in my principles, both in private and in my professional life?
- What steps am I taking for continual personal and professional growth?

- Do I feel a sense of integrity and self-respect when reflecting on my choices and behaviors?

Never Stop Learning

There is no such thing as a perfect leader.

We all have something to learn. It was Kenneth Blanchard, author of *The One Minute Manager,* who said, "When you stop learning, you stop growing."[19] And I agree! Most of the great servant leaders I know are constantly learning. They always have a book in their hand, a podcast they are listening to, or a leadership workshop they attend. They *know* they are not perfect, and they are continually striving to improve so they can be the most relevant and evolved leader for their teams.

The world of business is in a constant state of flux, with new technologies, shifting market dynamics, and evolving consumer preferences. A leader who actively engages in continuous learning is better equipped to help their teams navigate these changes. They can anticipate trends, adapt strategies accordingly, and guide their team through unchartered territories with confidence. Stagnant leaders, anchored in outdated methodologies and resistant to new ideas, preoccupied with their own priorities, find themselves ill-equipped to handle novel challenges or to innovate effectively, leading to missed opportunities and a decline in competitive edge.

In contrast, when team members see their leader actively seeking new knowledge and skills, it sets a powerful precedent.

---

19 (Blanchard, 2017)

It encourages a similar mindset among the team, promoting a learning environment where everyone is motivated to grow and contribute their best. Without it, both the leader and their team can collectively get stuck.

Employees look to their leaders for inspiration and guidance. A leader who is not growing or adapting can create a demotivating workplace atmosphere. This is currently rampant in the corporate world where leaders have been in the same position for 10-15 years but have done nothing to innovate that position or the team they led since the day they stepped into the leadership seat. They often create a rigid work environment that fails to respond effectively to market shifts or organizational challenges, leaving employees and the company itself ill-prepared to handle industry changes.

Chapter Wrap Up

On your journey to become a servant leader, remember:
- Start by slowing down and listening more.
- Reconnect with your authentic self in order to connect with others. Being consistently exactly who you are will make others trust you more and encourage them to be who they truly are.
- Remember the seven principles of a servant leader and try to embody them.
- Avoid being an unpredictable leader. Don't let outside distractions override your core values.

- Make consistent learning a priority. Never let yourself think you know everything you need to know.
- When mistakes happen, give candid and constructive feedback with clarity. This is one of the most significant ways you help your team grow.

Chapter 6:

Don't Mistake Kindness for Weakness

In corner offices, where the big decisions are made, kindness is often seen as a luxury at best and a liability at worst. Which leaves many corporate leaders with the impression that they should be tough, unyielding, and even ruthless. This is a skewed perception.

The truth is that kindness is not weakness.

On the top-rated Me-Suite podcast, hosted by my ex-colleague and friend Donna Peters, I had the privilege of discussing this very topic.

Donna is a highly accomplished former executive at Accenture, and with her podcast she has cultivated a platform where leaders share insights on applying strategic leadership in all facets of life. It currently rates top 1.5% of all podcast downloads globally and has a track record of 200+ fascinating interviews. The title "Me-Suite" is about the idea of managing your life with the same strategic focus and dedication as a C-Suite leader does in the boardroom. And she invited me onto her show during its first season.

Donna and I had previously worked together at AstraZeneca. I was part of the $12 billion US division of the (at that time) $33 billion global entity. Donna and I worked extensively together. She was a lead Accenture partner on several pivotal projects that I was leading, and our professional interactions left a lasting mutual impression of respect. On the podcast, Donna shared her recollection of our interactions, saying "I often felt when you and I were working together . . . I was the only person in the world because you were so focused on me."

This never would have happened, and I would not have left a lasting impression on Donna, if I hadn't committed myself to kindness and authenticity. And I likely would not have accepted the invitation to be interviewed on an untested podcast had I not been so convinced of Donna's depth and integrity. Donna is a values-based powerhouse individual whose trustworthiness and kindness are immediately obvious to all who are fortunate enough to work with her.

You, too, can have this type of impression on others if you embrace the strength behind kindness.

Even with authenticity and vulnerability as my core values, my kindness was never a weakness. I was often the most values-driven leader and the biggest advocate for my teams. But I was also frequently the person who let the most people go. That might sound like a contradiction, but it really isn't. I was the person who told people the bad news because I knew how to do it with kindness, and I knew how to respectfully offer the coaching they needed to achieve success.

When wielded wisely, kindness fosters an environment of trust and honesty. That doesn't mean leaders should be overly lenient or avoid tough decisions. That isn't kindness. Kindness still includes holding those we lead to a high standard and having expectations for them. It means we acknowledge that people have their own hopes, dreams, fears, and challenges, which honors the more human elements of work.

Sometimes, kind leaders are unfortunately viewed as not being "cut out" for the rough-and-tumble reality of corporate life. But in actuality, if a leader is emotionally intelligent enough to be kind, they are likely *more* qualified to be a leader.

When leaders embrace kindness, they unlock a powerful tool for building loyalty and commitment. Employees who feel valued and understood are more likely to be engaged, motivated, and aligned with the company's goals. Kindness doesn't diminish a leader's authority—it enhances it. Leaders who practice kindness show they are strong enough to be humane, confident enough to be empathetic, and wise enough to understand that the well-being of their team is integral to the success of the organization.

Coupled with a commitment to authenticity and high standards, kindness is without a doubt a powerful tool in a leader's arsenal.

Transparency Is Kind

Remember when we talked about removing your mask in chapter two? Doing so is part of being a kind leader. It was Brené Brown who said, "Clear is kind, unclear is unkind."[20]

---

20 (Brown, 2018)

When you're transparent with your thoughts and feelings, expressing them with kindness and respect, you provide a clear window for those you lead to understand who you are and what you stand for. In challenging situations like layoffs or difficult remediation conversations, transparency becomes even more critical. It's a humane and dignified approach that respects the other person's ability to handle the truth.

When I had to make tough decisions about letting people go, my focus was on being real and kind. I wanted to ensure that even in those tough moments, individuals were treated with dignity and had a clear understanding of the reason behind the decision. During one of the best-handled layoff scenarios I was part of (though they are never fun), we provided clear feedback including the strengths and talents of those being laid off and outplacement support to help them find a path forward. It was a lot of extra work, but it was worth it. Everyone we let go walked away with their head held high, and a plan for the future.

Transparency is fundamental to any company's health. Challenging layoff scenarios, poor results, and individual performance feedback all deserve clear communication. *Harvard Business Review* conducted a study that showed the effectiveness of transparency within the workplace. They found employees were 76% more engaged in a high-trust workplace.[21] Meaning lack of transparency adds to the disengagement we continually see across the corporate world.

---

21 (Zak, 2017)

Think back to that leader you want to embody. How do they communicate? When you take a microscope to their actions and language, you'll usually find they are highly transparent individuals.

When leadership consistently communicates openly about the company's goals, challenges, and changes, it sets a clear framework within which employees can align their expectations and efforts. This clarity helps in demystifying organizational objectives, enabling employees to understand the 'why" behind their immediate work and how their work contributes to the broader picture. Plus, it's a bonus that employees who are well-informed about their company's vision, strategies, and challenges are more likely to set realistic expectations for their roles and career progression.

Remember, a transparent culture is a thriving culture. Again, "clear is kind."

Nurturing Isn't Negative

In the traditional corporate playbook, nurturing gets a bad rap. We've been conditioned to believe in the virtues of a stiff upper lip, the relentless pursuit of goals, and the dismissal of what's labeled as "soft skills" (for example, emotional intelligence and the ability to connect with others on a human level). Luckily, this perception is starting to change. But it's still far behind what it should be.

Let me tell you, there is nothing "soft" about these skills. In fact, they are some of the most difficult to achieve, yet the most valuable and crucial competencies a leader can possess. When it comes to using these skills, authenticity, empathy, and kindness *are* the prerequisites. An authentic leader is nurturing and open, willing to take feedback and willing to give it.

Harvard Business Review's (*HBR*) article, "Creating the Best Workplace on Earth," emphasizes the significance of authenticity in leadership.[22] The research suggests that organizations thrive when they allow employees to be their genuine selves. By creating an environment where people feel safe and valued for who they are, leaders can unlock a level of engagement and creativity that rigid, traditional corporate environments often fail to achieve.

Leadership that genuinely makes a difference and leaves a lasting impact is inherently nurturing. When leaders prioritize the growth and well-being of their team members, it translates into a more cohesive and high-performing team. This isn't limited to female leaders. There was a time when nurturing was dismissively attributed to the female gender, but in truth, it's a leadership superpower that all leaders—men, women, and anyone else—should strive for.

6 Practical Ways to Imbue Kindness into Your Leadership

In my own journey, I have found several practical ways to include kindness in my leadership style. I have offered this advice to many leaders I have coached along the way, and now I want to offer it to

22 (Goffee & Jones, 2013)

Janice Jackson

you. Many of us in corporate leadership roles might not have had a nurturing leader to show us how to include kindness in our day-to-day management. Let these tactics act as an outline for you.

Not all of these tactics will resonate with everyone, but I hope at least some of them resonate with you and help you become a more nurturing and authentic leader today.

1. Treat Everyone as an Individual

Every team member is more than just a cog in the machine. They are individuals with unique strengths, challenges, and aspirations. As a leader, your first responsibility is to recognize and appreciate individuality. While tasks and deliverables are important, they should not overshadow team cohesiveness. The groundwork of successful task execution lies in a team that feels valued, understood, and supported.

A great example of this leadership style can be found in the television series *Ted Lasso*, which is a heartwarming, inspirational television show about Ted Lasso, an American college football coach who unexpectedly gets hired to coach a struggling English Premier League soccer team ("football" in the UK), despite having little knowledge of soccer. The series shows Ted's unorthodox coaching methods and his relentlessly positive attitude, which he uses to win over the skeptical team, its management, and its fans. Ted's folksy, upbeat demeanor and unflagging belief in the goodness of people stand in stark contrast to the cynicism and cutthroat nature of professional sports. His approach to leadership is captured well when he says, "For me, success is not about the wins and losses. It's about helping these young fellas be the best versions of themselves on and off the field."[23]

The true measure of leadership lies in the positive impact you have on individuals' lives, both professionally and personally. Be sure to treat everyone you meet as the individual they are and show that you truly see them.

2. Realize That People Have Lives Outside of Work

We all have priorities outside of work. Reporting to a leader who doesn't recognize that is one of the quickest ways for an individual to become disenfranchised and disconnected from a company.

Effective leadership recognizes that team members have lives filled with personal responsibilities, challenges, and relationships. When leaders show understanding and support for their team's personal needs—be it attending to children, spouses, or aging parents—they cultivate a deeper sense of loyalty and often witness a significant increase in productivity.

Now, this doesn't mean turning a blind eye to under-performance.

When someone consistently fails to meet expectations despite having all the necessary resources and support, tough decisions must be made. The goal is to maintain the integrity of the team. But you would be surprised how hard someone will work for you

---

23 (Lassoism, n.d.)

if you give them a couple accommodations to help them out of a tough situation.

3. Be Fair Across the Board

Every one of us has experienced a leader who prefers one person over another, and their preferences are clear. As a result, the favored person often gets away with more, has less strict rules at work, and might even avoid trouble due to their friendly relationship with the boss. Tell me, when this happened to you, how did you feel about the leader?

When you establish clear team agreements and adhere to them, you set a foundation for fairness. These agreements should encompass everything from work expectations to behavioral norms.

One common mistake I've observed among less effective leaders is their reluctance to address underperformance. They often overburden high-performing team members (the A-players) while allowing underperformers to slide by. This not only puts undue pressure on the top performers but also demoralizes them, leading to disenchantment within the team. It's crucial to understand that true kindness in leadership involves making difficult decisions for the greater good of the team.

When a leader is fair, it resonates throughout the team. Members feel respected and valued, leading to increased motivation and a more positive work environment. Conversely, when fairness is absent, it can lead to resentment, reduced productivity, and a toxic work culture. As a leader, your commitment to fairness in all interactions sets a powerful example for others to follow.

4. Prioritize People Management

As a leader, your primary role is to lead and develop people; tasks come second. This means actively engaging in the development of your team.

Many new leaders have a difficult time transitioning away from individual contributor work into management. In their previous positions, they were given a list of tasks to do and expected to execute them effectively. They likely performed this execution well, which got them into the leadership role. Unfortunately, this often means that when they step into this role, they are used to executing tasks, not focusing on the people. Most people are not trained on how to make that transition.

I have always been (and remain to this day) *stunned* by the number of companies that neglect to ensure ongoing leadership development of those they promote into managerial roles. But, sadly, even in 2024, this is still the case, which leaves leaders to take their own training into their own hands. The moment you get a direct report, people management should become your number one priority. You may need to seek out resources on how to do it well, but each of us should be aware of this fact before becoming leaders.

When you prioritize people management, that work is less tangible and often more difficult. There will be days when you feel like you have completed nothing on your to-do list, but members of your team will walk away feeling more supported and better equipped to do their job. To do this, I prefer quarterly reviews to help establish a people-first approach. Meeting once a year for annual reviews is never enough. Too much time passes between feedback, leaving direct reports to blindly hope they are doing well. Quarterly reviews strike a good balance between giving employees enough time to showcase their progress and providing timely feedback to keep them on track.

The goal is to establish a feedback loop that encourages growth and learning. This loop should be characterized by clarity and consistency, ensuring that no team member is left in the dark about their performance. Regular feedback sessions are opportunities for constructive dialogue, where both achievements and areas for improvement are discussed openly. After these feedback sessions, both you and the employee should be actively working on what was discussed.

They focus on deliverables; you focus on supporting them and encouraging key skills.

5. Make It a Habit to Observe Team Dynamics

As a leader, you need to have a finger on the pulse of your team dynamics. Keep an eye out for negative behaviors like finger-pointing, bullying, or passive-aggressive communication. These behaviors harm individual team members and erode the team's overall morale and productivity.

Ignoring these issues is not an option; they need to be addressed head-on.

This isn't about micromanaging but about understanding how your team interacts and collaborates. Are there underlying tensions? Do some members feel marginalized? Regular observation can help you identify and rectify these issues before they escalate.

For those of you at VP and C-level positions, make skip-level reviews a habit. Skip-level meetings are an effective way to gauge the effectiveness of a director or middle manager. By meeting with employees who are one or two levels below your direct reports, you get a clearer picture of the day-to-day operations and team dynamics. This exposes a leader who does well at "managing up" with a boss but doesn't treat their peers or direct reports well. These meetings can uncover issues that might not be visible at the higher levels and provide insights into areas that need improvement. In my earlier senior roles, I learned this the hard way. I was slow in spotting those middle-managers who were very good at "managing up," and it cost us morale and valuable talent.

Don't let this happen to your team.

6. Make Quarterly Team Workshops a Priority

I'm a big believer in workshops.

Think about the way you feel when you step out of a good workshop. It brings back a little of that "change the world" feeling that comes from exciting beginnings, doesn't it? We feel invigorated and ready to tackle our projects. Our minds are buzzing with exciting new ideas, and we want to jump in headfirst. This is a *good* thing and will only serve your team.

Workshops help us as leaders break down barriers and encourage our teams to think differently.

A workshop every quarter can help your team avoid getting stuck in ruts. They shouldn't be viewed as optional or secondary to daily tasks. They are essential for the team's growth and cohesion and should be treated that way. To ensure these workshops are productive, establish ground rules regarding distractions like phone calls, emails, or side-talking. Make it clear that during the workshop, the focus should be entirely on the activities and discussions at hand. Emphasize that in this space, all ideas are welcomed and valued.

The content of these workshops can vary, covering topics like team purpose, aligning with the company's mission, recognition or even conducting DiSC assessments. The goal is to encourage team members to step back and think about the bigger picture, interact in new ways, and understand each other better. Workshops that involve interactive elements, like role-playing or group discussions, are particularly effective in breaking down walls and stimulating new ideas.

Keep in mind, while these workshops don't need to be lengthy or held off-site, changing the environment can be beneficial. It helps create a mental and physical space distinct from daily work pressures. However, even if conducted in the office, the key is to create an atmosphere where team members feel comfortable being in the present, expressing themselves, and exploring new concepts.

Kindness Is One of the Hardest Things to Do

One final note on kindness. I'll say it: being genuinely kind as a leader can be difficult. Committing to kindness might be one of the hardest things you will do in your leadership journey. But it is also one of the things that will make you a more powerful leader. The goal is to understand the complex reality of human interactions, to have the courage to step out of your comfort zone, and to bring out the best in others.

This is not a passive or easy process; it demands courage, patience, intentionality, and resilience.

Chapter Wrap Up

Remember, when intentionally incorporating kindness into your leadership style:

- Transparency is kind, even in difficult situations.
- Every leader, whether they are male or female, can and should focus on nurturing their team.
- There are several practical ways you can include kindness in your leadership style. Pick a few that resonate the most with you and be intentional about practicing them.

- Remember that kindness is not, and never will be, weakness.
- Find ways to understand the more human realities of professional relationships. The more you understand this, the more you can help your team connect and grow.

Chapter 7:

Question the Norms

I firmly believe norms are meant to be challenged.

In business, when trying to implement something new, we often hear "we have always done it this way." But this is a quick way to stifle innovation. A process can always be improved, especially as technology and society evolves. If you want to be a standout leader and make a positive difference in the lives of people you manage, and consequently in your company results, then you should absolutely question the norms placed before you.

This takes a great deal of critical thinking. It's easy to get a process handed to you and then continue to follow the same steps that others have before you. After all, it has worked in the past, hasn't it? Why should it need to be changed? It's much harder to look at a process critically and ask the right questions to find out if it is the most efficient it could be.

Leadership norms are no different. It's easy to accept these norms and assume that they are ideal, simply because other generations before us have followed them. But in truth, many of the norms we face in the corporate world were designed for an outdated context and are damaging to innovation.

If you want to make a difference as a leader, you need to challenge these norms. I know I certainly did. And my career and those who worked with me are better for it. To get you started, here is a list of the leadership norms I refused to accept.

Norm to Challenge: Prioritizing Tasks over People Management

Too often, leaders are promoted into management roles because of their prowess in a specific task, not for their leadership skills. This encourages them to focus on task management instead of team management.

But neglecting team management leads to misalignment, where team members veer off in different directions, creating more issues that could have been avoided with upfront, collaborative planning. It's a vicious cycle we see consistently within the corporate world. More focus is put on task management, creating micromanagers who care more about the tasks people perform and less about the people.

The number one priority in management should be the development of people. The more you invest in aligning and organizing your team, the more efficient their task execution becomes because everyone is rowing in the same direction. But if you remain task-focused, and just bark instructions, you miss the opportunity to develop individual abilities and to benefit from potentially outstanding results that come from cohesive effort. Many think the people management aspect of your role diminishes as you climb higher in the corporate hierarchy, but that *couldn't be further from the truth*. As a new manager, people management might constitute about 20% of your job, but as a Vice President or Chief Executive, the proportion of time and effort you dedicate to people management should be closer to 70% of your job.

Micromanagement is a crime against humanity! Ditch it. It doesn't serve you, it doesn't serve the individuals you are managing, and it doesn't serve the company.

Norm to Challenge: Bigger Title, Less Accessibility

Often, the higher up the ladder a leader climbs, the less accessible they become to those they manage.

This shouldn't be the case. True leadership is about being more accessible as you gain seniority, not less. You can't delegate tasks and goals from an isolated office. You need to be on the ground, visible, and actively involved. There is a significant gap between talking about company values and actually living them. Too often, leaders profess commitment to these values but then retreat behind closed doors, becoming unapproachable and disconnected from their team's reality.

Now, if you are a senior leader, you might be thinking, "But Janice, my day is booked from beginning to end all the time." Trust me, I've been there. As you rise in the ranks of corporate leadership, your time becomes increasingly consumed by meetings, strategic planning sessions, and decision-making processes. Which often leads to leaders that are physically present but functionally absent from their teams. I know the stresses you are battling and that you likely have a to-do list with hundreds of items on it.

But, to truly inspire and lead, you need to flip this norm on its head.

I'm not saying this is easy. And it certainly won't happen naturally. You can't just by happenstance be visible or approachable. You have to deliberately carve out time in your day when people know they can approach you, whether that means booking open office time or choosing to walk around and have a chat with people. Whatever the mechanism, you need to be intentional about it and plan it. If you leave it to fate, you will be in never-ending meetings with other executives, and nobody on your team will see you.

Being intentional about availability means actively managing your schedule to prevent it from being overrun with executive-level meetings and responsibilities. I found blocking time in my calendar where I was available to my team was the best way I could do this. I fiercely protected that time when my peers tried to grab it back. This battle is *worth* it because connection with you is key to your team's success.

Norm to Challenge: What the Boss Says Goes

As a professional aiming to make a real impact, you should be wary of falling into the trap of blind acceptance. "What the boss says goes" is a cop-out. It's easy to just accept their words and move on without applying critical thinking to a task. But, if you want to be a standout leader, you need to embrace your role as a contributor of meaningful ideas, not as an executor of tasks.

Start by recognizing that every directive or established method is an opportunity for enhancement. This is where you can begin to differentiate yourself as a bold and innovative thinker. The key here is to approach this with respect, optimism, and enthusiasm and to demonstrate this approach to the wider team. By role-modeling professional, respectful, constructive questioning, you also ensure that your team maintains the same kind of healthy mutual respect with you. The last thing you want as a leader is to be surrounded by sycophants. It is the fastest way to be blind-sided by internal or external challenges that could be fatal to your career and to your team or company success.

When you propose changes or new ideas, do it in a way that is constructive, not confrontational. Instead of dismissing the old ways outright, acknowledge their value and suggest additions or improvements. Rather than saying, "This method is outdated; we should scrap it," try framing it as, "This method has worked well; I wonder if we can make it even more effective by . . ." This approach shows respect for past efforts and demonstrates your commitment to collective progress.

Your goal is to be seen as a positive force for change, someone who respects existing achievements while eagerly exploring opportunities for improvement. Always approach these situations with the assumption that there's more to learn.

Norm to Challenge: The Boss Knows Everything

The leader of a team doesn't need to know everything about that department or project to be an effective leader. An orchestra conductor doesn't need to know how to play every instrument to do their jobs well. Instead, their expertise lies in understanding how to bring out the best in each musician, ensuring that all the parts come together harmoniously. Just as a leader's strength doesn't lie in knowing everything, but in their ability to orchestrate a team's talents and skills to achieve the best possible results.

Too often, leaders think they have to pretend they know everything. The misconception that leaders should have encyclopedic knowledge about every detail can create unrealistic expectations and pressures. Talk about a quick way to burnout!

When leaders operate from a place of fear and try to appear invincible, they inadvertently stifle the potential of their team. They miss out on the diverse insights and ideas that team members can offer. But by showing vulnerability and openness, leaders can foster a culture where team members feel safe to voice their thoughts, offer solutions, and actively participate in the project's success.

I have firsthand experience with this. I once led an IT department, even though my prior experience was leading marketing and sales. I certainly wasn't an expert in tech processes. And pretending to would be a quick way of putting on a mask and denying my authentic self. So, I was very clear with what I did know and what I didn't know, and I made it a priority to *listen*.

I started by gathering the IT VPs and Directors together with the CTO. While we were all together, I explained the goal that we had been asked to achieve by our global headquarters, and why the new software and systems were required to align our processes with the rest of the company to achieve future efficiencies and profitability. Then, I invited the entire IT leadership team to outline a potential pathway and timeline as well as needed resources to achieve the deliverable. We then collectively presented our strategy to the visiting headquarter team and collaborated with them to hammer out the plan.

Once this was done, we could all move forward with a collective vision and a sense of ownership. The result was a highly successful technological implementation that was on budget and on time. Because I involved the right people from the very beginning, I avoided being the kind of leader that barks directions to a team without hearing and understanding their concerns, questions, and recommendations. Instead, we worked together to create a shared path we could all deliver on.

Leaders who find themselves in positions like this one need to resist the urge to feign expertise. If the context and early inclusive planning is ignored for the sake of looking like you know it all, the results will suffer every time. It's far more effective and inspiring to lead with humility and openness about your strengths and areas where you have less expertise. Acknowledging that you don't have all the answers encourages team members to step up, share their expertise, and contribute more significantly to the project. In these scenarios, your role as a leader is *not* to have all the answers, but to be an effective facilitator and advocate for solution-oriented ideas from the team.

Norm to Challenge: Continuous Work Equals Productivity

It's a common misconception that long hours and constant work leads to better results. However, true productivity requires a balanced approach, leaving room for creativity and thoughtful deliberation.

During a project, I recommend spending the first 15% of the entire allocated timeline ensuring everyone understands the project's needs, its alignment with company strategy, their individual roles, how success will be measured, behavioral guidelines, and the targets. This work might feel like delaying the start of the project. But, in reality, getting these elements right from the start significantly reduces the likelihood of misunderstandings and the need for rework later. You will be amazed to find how many times teams are overworked and burnt out simply because the critical components of the project haven't been well established upfront. If management hasn't yet defined what they really want, rework or new work will be demanded at the last minute.

Sound familiar? Every one of us has had a leader who does this. Who demands new materials or reworked files in the eleventh hour right before a launch or release. Do you remember how that feels? That stressful sense of overwhelm that overtakes you as you try to do an impossible task quickly. It's unnecessary stress. Sure, it's continuous work—sure, you *look* productive—but all it actually does is foster burnout.

To avoid this, always nail down the critical components mentioned above and establish and continually reassess efficient processes. These processes should be designed to serve both the team and the company, with clear milestones and sign-off points. Well-designed processes help avoid the chaos of last-minute changes and the stress of rework. If these processes are well designed *and adhered to*, this stops a lot of the last-minute rework busyness.

If you can't or won't do this first 15% of the process, you shouldn't be a leader.

Your teams won't be productive. Especially if you are the type of person to regularly say you want something on Friday night and expect it on Monday morning. Which is unfair. Be the leader who refuses to do this to your team.

Norm to Challenge: You Can Have High Quality and Speed at Low Cost

This trifecta—quality, speed, and low cost—is a balancing act in project management. The reality is, prioritizing one or two of these aspects inevitably impacts the others. You simply can't have it all, and there are trade-offs that need to be made.

A colleague of mine, a top player in the product development industry with experience at giants like J&J and Procter & Gamble, used to say that when it comes to quality, speed, or low cost, "You can have two, but you can't have all three."

Many managers aim for the stars, wanting to achieve the impossible without being practical about what it takes to set their employees up for success. The result? They end up overloading their best performers, leading to high turnover, demoralized teams, and diminished results. As a leader, it's your responsibility to decide which of these three aspects are most crucial for a particular project.

If cost-effectiveness is the priority, outsourcing might be a solution, but this could impact quality or timing. If you are managing a high-quality brand, compromising on quality is not an option, so you might need to adjust timelines or budgets accordingly. This is where you need to consider what truly matters to your customers and what has been established within your brand. When faced with demands for high quality, rapid delivery, and low cost all at once, it's vital to be skeptical and question the strategic thinking (or lack thereof) behind those demands. Push back against the notion that all three can be achieved simultaneously.

Norm to Challenge: Because You Are a Visionary, You Should Lead

There is a widespread belief that creative and visionary individuals naturally make great managers. But not every creative genius is cut out for leadership roles.

A prime example, as highlighted in a New York Times article[24], is Steve Jobs, the co-founder of Apple. Jobs was undoubtedly a pioneer, a man whose vision revolutionized multiple industries. Yet, his leadership style was often described as abrasive and demanding. Jobs' approach, though effective in driving innovation, was not always conducive to a positive work environment. He was known for his blunt criticism and high expectations, which, while pushing the boundaries of technological advancement, sometimes came at the cost of employee morale and job satisfaction. Yes, I hear you saying, "Jobs was by any measure successful!" But I put it to you that he would have achieved *more* success (monetary and personal) had he attended more to the human side of the leadership equation.

Skills in a particular domain do not automatically translate into effective management or leadership excellence. What makes you exceptional at your trade does not mean you can inspire, guide, and elevate a team. Companies that promote purely on this basis are doing a disservice to themselves and to everyone involved— especially to the unfortunate souls who find themselves reporting to a leader who is ill-equipped to lead.

I vividly remember reporting to a visionary, charismatic marketer whose skills were clear and had led to significant achievements within the company. He was promoted based on merit to lead the entire marketing division. Unfortunately, he didn't have the people management skills or ability to inspire and lead a team, so he ended up in the weeds, micromanaging

---

24 (New York Times, n.d.)

and dictating, leading to the disillusionment and ultimately disengagement of the teams. Not only did team morale suffer, but turnover increased, short- and long-term goals went unachieved, and the bottom line sank.

Visionary individuals are assets to any organization, thanks to their ability to dream big and think outside the box. However, their talents don't always translate well into managing people. They might be fantastic at coming up with innovative ideas, but their tendency to frequently change directions can result in high expenses and frustrated teams. In my opinion, the best way to harness the genius of a visionary is to partner them with a strong leader.

There should be a clear distinction between being a visionary and being a people manager.

People who have been promoted based on their domain-specific skills should only be put in charge if they possess the necessary leadership skills *and* are provided the training to develop them. More often than not, what's lacking in corporate leadership is a comprehensive evaluation of an individual's readiness and suitability to lead others. This puts them in a position where they likely won't find success and could actually harm the individuals they manage.

For those without inherent leadership qualities, there should be a different avenue for progression. There are a few companies out there who are already doing this. They promote individuals on two different paths, the "I Path" (Individual Contributor) and the "M Path" (Management). The former allows for promotions, higher salaries, and more senior titles without the responsibility of overseeing others. This way, you don't compromise someone's career or mental well-being due to lack of leadership skills. The latter path promotes those who have the necessary emotional intelligence skills (EQ) needed for management. Once this dual promotional path is in place, companies are far less likely to hamper their progress with mediocre management and disengaged, disillusioned employees.

I recall a truly exceptional technical contributor in one of my organizations. He neither displayed people management skills nor indicated any interest in developing himself as a leader, so his department head and I recognized his excellence as an individual contributor and compensated him accordingly. He was thriving, but in the long run, he ended up moving away due to his fiancée's job and accepted a leadership role in another company. Unfortunately, he is struggling, and his direct reports are struggling even more. He shows little patience for training or helping employees see the big picture, and if they ask a specific question, he provides a specific answer and no more. You can just imagine where this will lead.

Many of us want managerial roles because they are the only paths we have to more money or bigger titles. But once we get there, we realize we don't like having to manage people. And this is okay! Not everyone wants to lead a team or shoulder the responsibility of a C-suite leader. This shouldn't be the only promotional path available to you.

To unlock the full potential of both individuals and teams, companies need to be more discerning when promoting employees to leadership roles by offering "I Path" promotional tracks. Only then will we start to mend the disconnect between the qualifications for doing a job well and the skills needed to lead others effectively.

Norm to Challenge: New Hires Are Less Respected Than Senior Workers

The traditional hierarchy of seniority, where the input and perspectives of longer tenured or higher-ranking employees are given more weight than those of newer employees, often overlooks valuable perspectives that newer employees bring to the table. Which is a fancy way of saying that a seniority-based hierarchy is outdated and doesn't necessarily serve a company well.

Technological advancements and societal norms are evolving at lighting speed. The input of the younger generations is indispensable. They bring with them a pulse on the latest trends, and they have a knack for innovation because of their unique understanding of modern consumer behavior.

Dismissing their contributions simply because of their "junior" status in the company is unwarranted *and* a strategic oversight.

A company's ability to stay relevant and competitive hinges on its capacity to harness diverse perspectives. This includes tapping into the rich reservoir of ideas from employees at different life stages and levels of experience.

For instance, in one of the companies where I had a leadership role, we recognized the need for diversity of thought in our advisory boards. By rotating members and including voices from both seasoned leaders and newcomers, we ensured a constant flow of fresh, dynamic ideas. This prevented stagnation and provided a more accurate reflection of our diverse customer base. We achieved hyper-growth and leap-frogged many of our competitors who ended up floundering by limiting their customer input to advisors who had been around a long time and were advocating outdated practices.

This is especially relevant in an era where global markets and rapid technological changes demand adaptability and a multifaceted approach to decision-making. Companies that recognize and harness the power of diverse perspectives set themselves up for greater profitability and long-term success.

Plus, you might be surprised at the great ideas your newer players bring to the table.

Embrace Change

I'm not the first to say this, and I won't be the last, but it's the truth. Change is uncomfortable, and it always will be. But addressing and challenging the norms that stifle innovation is how leaders help companies become better.

Think about how the COVID-19 pandemic reshaped our perspectives on how important it is to be in office when performing a job. For years, we all believed that being physically present in an office was crucial for productivity and collaboration. The norm was clear: work happens at the office. However, the pandemic forced a global reconsideration of this belief. Suddenly, organizations worldwide found themselves re-evaluating the necessity of traditional office spaces. As a result, the adoption of remote and hybrid work models accelerated, challenging long-held assumptions about work environments.

The shift to remote and hybrid work models, born out of necessity, has debunked long-standing myths about productivity and work environments. It's shown us that many jobs can be completed as well (if not better) at any location, allowing for companies to draw from a wider range of talent and employees to find more work-life balance.

As leaders and professionals, our response to change defines us. Embracing change isn't just about keeping up; it's about leading the way.

Chapter Wrap Up

Questioning norms is a must. Here are a few key things to keep in mind:

- Being a leader means being available to your team, no matter your title.
- Be a positive force for challenging norms. Your contributions are important. Model this behavior for your team.
- Don't be afraid to admit when you don't know something—it will actually help your standing with your team.

- Help your team understand all aspects of a project up front to avoid rework or continuous work. Do the first 15%!
- When it comes to high quality, speed, or low cost, remember you can't have it all. Prioritize based on your brand and customer.
- If you are a visionary, you need to look inward honestly and analyze if you would be a good leader or if you should stick to an individual contributor role.
- Every team member, new or senior, has ideas that can help a company innovate.
- Be a leader who embraces change.

Chapter 8:

Don't Let the Assholes Derail You

Every one of us has experienced an asshole or two at work.

For me, it was while I worked at a fast-growing company around the billion-dollar mark. This company was on a trajectory of hyper-growth and doing remarkably well. However, despite its success, there were a couple of fundamental flaws in its structure—a toxic advisory board that lacked depth and diversity in experience, and a visionary CEO with no leadership experience.

Our CEO, a classic visionary, was charming and creative. The company achieved outstanding results while he was partnered with a Co-CEO who possessed excellent people management skills. However, after the departure of his partner, our CEO lacked the discipline and leadership skills to prevent the toxic element of his advisory board from having a very poisonous effect on the company. As the Chief Brand Officer, I found myself in the eye of the storm when the company decided to launch a new product category. My team and I dove deep into development and research, gathering global input and ensuring diverse feedback.

Based on those results, we put a plan together. But as we neared the launch, the toxic individuals within the advisory group grew apprehensive. They feared moving away from the company's roots would endanger its future, despite our extensive research indicating otherwise and despite our efforts to reassure them.

They set up a meeting, and the group aggressively targeted me. It was clear they were hesitant to confront the CEO about their concerns, so they tore me and my team's plan apart in that meeting. They were not kind. Despite the CEO's horror at the situation, he couldn't counter the monster he had unwittingly created. It was a moment that left the entire room in shock. A senior executive from Australia shared that he would now do everything in his power to persuade his daughter not to pursue a career in the corporate world given the outrageous behavior he had just witnessed. The rest of the Advisory Board members decried the actions of the toxic group and demanded apologies.

That meeting crossed a boundary for me. It was harsh and cruel, and I knew my team and I didn't deserve it. I took a week off to take a trip with my daughter to reflect on the discussion and returned with my resignation. The decision wasn't easy given the usual considerations we all have . . . mortgage to pay, children in school, etc. But a line had been crossed, and I couldn't continue in an environment where such toxicity was tolerated.

In my final discussions with the CEO, he finally agreed to accept my decision, and I agreed to stay on for eight weeks to ensure a smooth transition. It was important to me not to leave the company, or the CEO, in the lurch because I wanted to resign with grace and on my own terms. The event was egregious and there were apologies and compensation. But I knew I couldn't stay. Even though I didn't have another opportunity lined up, I made it clear what I would accept and what I wouldn't.

And it's not just me—we've all been there, in toxic situations where boundaries are overstepped and lines are crossed. Maybe not on such a grand scale, but in ways that shake our confidence and challenge our principles. In these moments, where we feel undermined, undervalued, or simply caught in the crossfire of corporate politics, our resolve is tested. These are the moments to dig deep, listen to your inner voice, and act accordingly.

Don't Say Yes Just to Please

In the workplace, we are always trying to please. We want to get the next promotion, we hope to have a good track record with the boss, and we like the praise that comes from being one of the top players. But the result often leaves us stretched too thin. We end up struggling with our responsibilities because we have too much on our plate.

Always saying yes isn't doing you any favors. In fact, biting off more than you can chew is a bit like telling a white lie. If you agree to finish a project by Friday simply because the boss demands it, with no consideration as to whether you actually have time for said project, you might miss the deadline. Then you become the person nobody wants to be in the office—the one who drops the ball and can't be trusted.

Instead, be real about what you can handle. It might feel awkward, especially if you're the type who hates to say no. But honesty goes a long way. It shows you're reliable and, more importantly, self-aware and accountable. Plus, it's a relief not to juggle more than you can handle, and you will do better work with a more balanced workload.

Leaders might come to you with hard deadlines and high demands, but poor planning is not an excuse for unreasonable or last-minute demands to be placed on your shoulders.

I coach an individual who was told to criticize a vendor for not meeting expectations. But she didn't agree because the expectations were never clearly set for the vendor by leadership. So instead of just saying yes, she crafted a respectful, straightforward email where she pointed out that the vendor couldn't be blamed for missing the mark if they never knew where the mark was to begin with.

And she was terrified to send it.

She confided in me that she was worried she would be looked down on or criticized because she didn't simply "do what the boss said." I reminded her that if her honest constructive feedback wasn't welcomed, then maybe this company wasn't the right place for her. It's a harsh truth, but in a healthy work environment your ideas and concerns should be heard, not ignored.

So, she sent the email. And to her surprise, her leader agreed with her and appreciated that she pointed this out to him. By standing her ground and communicating effectively, she resolved the issue, and she found an ally in her boss.

Pleasing for the sake of pleasing should be banned from our personal repertoire. It doesn't help the company, and it doesn't help you become a standout leader. In the book *Brave, Not Perfect*, Reshma Saujani discusses how many of us, especially women, are raised to please and be perfect instead of being brave. She says, "We've become conditioned to compromise and shrink ourselves in order to be liked. The problem is, when you work so hard to get everyone to like you, you very often end up not liking yourself so much."[25]

It takes bravery to gently say no when you can't meet a deadline or have too much on your plate. But without that bravery, we aren't being honest with ourselves, with our co-workers, or with our leaders. The focus should be on being genuine and authentic, rather than conforming to the stereotype of being a "yes man" or a "yes woman." Believe it or not, doing so will make you stand out *more* in the workplace, not less.

Listen to Your Gut

When something happens that jars us and has potentially crossed a line, many of us are extremely good at talking ourselves out of frustration and disappointment. We think we did something to deserve the treatment, or we could have said something to prevent it. We even talk ourselves into thinking we are being too dramatic if we get upset or angry at a clear boundary being crossed.

---

25 (Saujani, 2019)

When you feel a boundary gets crossed, and your gut clenches, reminding you that this is a hard boundary you have set, *do not* talk yourself out of it. Do not rationalize the situation or dismiss it. Your intuition is a powerful indicator of when things are not aligning with your core values and goals, and you should not ignore it.

Ask yourself, does this situation respect your worth? Does it contribute positively to your personal development? If you find yourself deviating from your intended path just to conform to a toxic norm, it's time to reassess. You deserve an environment that fosters growth, not one that stifles it.

Not every situation will present a clear scenario. But, if you find yourself constantly on the losing end, it's a sign to take action. Staying in a toxic work environment is like being stuck in a petri dish of negativity and hoping that negativity will go away. In truth, the negativity will only grow.

If the harmful elements persist and you choose to stay, the situation will likely deteriorate. You deserve a work environment that nurtures your talents and respects your individuality, not one that drains your spirit and hampers your progress.

So, listen to your gut when it tells you something is wrong.

How to Know When to Leave Your Job (And How to Do It Well)

Making the decision to leave a toxic job can be tough, but you need to do what's best for you on your terms. *If you are still earning, learning, and growing despite the existence of some toxic individuals, you are progressing and can afford to stay a little longer.* However, if progression has stalled, and if you are sure you have given it your all and tried to resolve the situation with no improvement, it's okay to prioritize your well-being. Skilled and valuable employees are always in demand, so don't undervalue yourself by staying in a negative situation.

If the toxic environment is harming your confidence, spirit, and self-respect, it's a clear sign that you need to remove yourself from that situation. You have options: you can start looking for a new job while you're still employed, you can work on establishing your own freelance or consulting business, or you might choose to quit first and then focus on your future.

The key point here is recognizing when it's time to move on for the sake of your mental and emotional health. Staying in a harmful environment can take a significant toll on your confidence and overall well-being. Remember, your career path should be a source of growth and satisfaction, not a drain on your spirit and self-respect.

Imagine you are in a situation with a difficult boss or a toxic colleague. You have tried to address the issues head-on. You have used all the steps we talked about in Chapter Four on what to do when someone ignores your boundaries. And through all this, you have been truthful and transparent and have maintained your integrity. Yet, you still aren't heard, or you find the situation escalating. If you have communicated your concerns as constructively, unemotionally, and professionally as possible, yet find no resolution or change, it's a sign to reevaluate your position. When your work environment is no longer in harmony with who you are and what you believe in, staying can do more harm than good, both to your professional growth and personal well-being.

Your situation is no longer in alignment with you, and you are no longer in alignment with it.

When it becomes clear that your current job no longer aligns with your values and aspirations, it's time to initiate a thoughtful and purpose-driven career transition. This begins with preparing yourself for new opportunities. Start by polishing your resume and LinkedIn profile, ensuring they reflect your latest achievements and skills. Communicate with your network confidently, letting them know you're open to new challenges and opportunities.

Even if you find yourself in a less-than-ideal situation, remember the value of earning, learning, and growing. These aspects can keep you moving forward while you search for a new position or venture into setting up your own business or pursuing a dream. The goal is not to escape a bad situation hastily but to transition towards a healthier culture and more fulfilling work, that resonates with your purpose.

In today's world, brimming with opportunities for side gigs and self-made income, the avenues to explore your passions and skills are vast and varied. Take time to do some introspective work. Assess your strengths, interests, and what you genuinely would love to do. Is there an opportunity out there that aligns with your aspirations? Could your hobby or passion project evolve into a viable career path? And don't underestimate the power of volunteering and community involvement. These activities not only enrich your life but can also lead to valuable connections and unexpected career opportunities. Your network can be leveraged to open the door to different positions.

But, waiting might not always be an option. There is a time when staying in a toxic job environment becomes more detrimental than leaving it without a safety net. If you find that your job is draining your spirit and confidence, it's a clear signal that it's time to leave. Enduring a situation where your self-esteem and enthusiasm are being eroded can trap you in a downward spiral that affects your well-being and diminishes your prospects of securing future opportunities.

While financial stability is important, compromising your mental and emotional health for the sake of a paycheck is rarely worth it. The cost to your spirit and self-worth can be far greater.

Think about it like this: if you manage to step away from that toxic job while you've still got your confidence and self-belief intact, you are going to shine in your next job interviews. You'll walk in there knowing your worth and what you bring to the table, and trust me, it shows. But if you stick around in a draining, soul-sucking job for too long, it starts to chip away at your confidence. You don't want to reach a point where you start doubting your own abilities, right? Make that move before it gets to you.

Leave with Grace

When you've made the decision to leave, aim to do so with grace and dignity. This means avoiding public outbursts or burning bridges, no matter how tempting it might be to voice your frustrations. Consider the long-term impact of your actions. The professional world can be surprisingly small, and a graceful exit leaves a positive, lasting impression on those who matter.

But most of all, it shows your character, because you refuse to stoop to a level of behavior that is beneath you.

Resign professionally by giving the appropriate notice and, if possible, offering to assist in the transition period. Remember that leaving a toxic situation opens new doors to opportunities where your talents and skills will be better appreciated and utilized. A positive and respectful departure sets the stage for new beginnings so you can move forward with confidence.

Chapter Wrap Up

You deserve better than to be derailed by assholes. Remember:

- Don't say yes just to please. It isn't doing you or others any favors, and it truly is a form of dishonesty.
- Standing up for a broken boundary takes courage, but it's worth it, even if it means you leave a company.
- Leave with grace, even in hard circumstances. Harming or attacking the company or burning personal bridges only serves to drag you down and rarely has the desired result.

- If assholes are tolerated and persist, you aren't stuck. Consider your next move carefully.
- If you need to leave, then leave. No job should drain your spirit. If you stay in this position, it will be harder to get out of it due to the downward spiral that leads to a lack of confidence and trauma.

Chapter 9:

Watch Out for the Patriarchy

Many of us shy away from this conversation. It's difficult to have without pointing fingers or hurting feelings. But the reality is that the patriarchy does exist, and we have to realize how it might affect someone's view of the world. It might not look the same as it did fifty years ago. Especially because the pay gap has narrowed (though it's far from truly equal), and women have more rights than they used to.

But in truth, this problem hasn't gone away—it is just harder to identify.

My father was an academic and an intellectual, and I was lucky to have his influence in my life. He didn't see me or my brother's genders as a reason to treat us differently. He raised us as equals. So, I was relatively advanced in my career before I even noticed there was a difference in opportunity between men and women.

This difference became most obvious as I reached leadership roles. As I climbed higher up the corporate ladder, I had fewer and fewer female peers. Despite being equally competent and, in many cases, better suited for certain roles, women in leadership positions were rare. The more glaring this disparity became, the more I found that I was the lone female in the room. My experience in this isn't unique.

Even in industries where the products are exclusively for women, they are often marketed by men. I noticed that sanitary products, a quintessentially female product if ever there was one, are overseen by male brand, marketing, and sales managers. Talk about a disconnect between your leadership and your customer base!

Of course, I'm not saying we haven't seen *any* change. Women are gradually climbing the ladder and securing more middle and senior leadership positions. But it hasn't resolved the problem of the patriarchy. That will take years of unraveling and a lot more work than I can put into one chapter.

What I can do is help you recognize the problem and offer some tools to deal with it.

It's There, But It's Hard to Identify

Calling out the patriarchy can feel like grasping at smoke. Though we still see and can point to a disparity in pay—according to data from the Pew Research Center in 2022, it was found that for every dollar earned by a man in America, a woman earned only 82 cents[26]—much more is happening that we can't quite name.

To define it, the patriarchy is a system of power where masculinity is revered, and authority is often concentrated in the hands of men. Its presence is felt by women in the subtleties: the

---

26 (Aragao, 2023)

missed opportunities, the half-hearted listening to your ideas, the talking over you in meetings, and the selective invitations that subtly exclude. We have all seen it, heard it, and felt it. If you are a woman, you have likely experienced it for yourself. If you are a man, you likely have a mother, sister, wife, or friend who has told you a story about it. Sometimes it's blatant, like sharing an idea in a meeting which doesn't get heard until a male colleague repeats your words (don't you hate it when that happens?). But most of the time it is quiet, and it might not be obvious at first.

Each one of us has been affected by the patriarchy in one way or another. It can be an intangible force that has tangible impacts on your career and well-being. And while some of us may want to avoid it, or ignore it, and say, "Well, it doesn't affect my team, so I don't have to worry about it," you are likely wrong. The best—and only—way you can tackle this issue is to be on the lookout for it constantly.

But if it's intangible, how do you recognize it?

I've heard this question many times throughout my career as I have encouraged others to help tackle this problem. The best advice I can give is to check in with yourself. If something happens, and if it twists your gut but you are not sure why or if you should speak up, ask yourself these questions:

- Would my dad or brother be happy I was treated like this?
- Would my previous good boss be happy about me being treated about this?
- Would my spouse be okay with me being treated like this?
- Does this treatment align with my personal values?

If the answer is no to any of these questions, do something about it!

Addressing these issues correctly can be hard. No one wants to speak up and risk angering those above or around you. For this, I have two pieces of advice.

First, if you do speak up constructively and kindly, and you get punished for it, that company is not the place for you. Second, try the positivity sandwich. Which looks like this: "I really like what individual A is trying to achieve, but I don't feel as if individual A is taking the opportunity to include individual B, who has important contributions. Let's chat about that. I'm excited to see what the two individuals can achieve once they work out this challenge together." Another option would be to say, "What I really appreciate about you is X, what I saw went wrong on this occasion is Y, and I think if we work on that you'll be unstoppable."

This might sound manipulative, but if it's the truth, it's not manipulative—instead, it is tactful diplomacy. Often, this type of language is the best way to ensure that the lines of communication stay as open and positive as possible. If you only attack when approaching him a problem, people put their walls up. But if you acknowledge the positives, then point out the negatives, you will experience a much more open conversation. Constructive feedback is the key here. Before we can make change happen, we have to make sure those with whom we need to discuss these issues don't shut down. The moment you attack or get angry, they *will* stop hearing you.

If you are a leader, be the ally for women on your team. Ensure their voices are heard and their contributions recognized. Be on the lookout for biases that get in the way of qualified work. When your team sees you making a point of doing this, they will too.

Acting Like a Man Isn't the Answer

Women in the corporate world often face a struggle with authenticity and assertiveness because masculine norms are the expectation.

Late into my career, I was one of two females on the board of a global company, which was owned by an older and bigger parent company. And the parent company was very . . . patriarchal.

In this situation, my colleague and I found our initial years to be rewarding. We achieved promotional success and contributed significantly to the company's growth and innovation. But it gradually became clear there was a limit to how much we could contribute. We were valued, but only to a certain extent. The higher leadership of the company, which was governed by a group of men that had long held the reins, viewed us almost affectionately. As long as we didn't aim too high or challenge the status quo too vigorously, they were happy with us. It was clear that while they appreciated our contributions, they didn't take our aspirations seriously.

As time passed, we realized that our journey within the company had a ceiling. Despite our achievements and potential, it became increasingly apparent that any further advancement was unlikely, as the leadership consistently chose to elevate men over equally or more qualified women. Faced with this realization, my colleague and I chose to leave.

Our departures weren't dramatic, but we were not content with stagnation, so we sought opportunities elsewhere. The aftermath of our departure was telling. The company, while maintaining its approach of not letting women get too high within leadership, began to lose other talented women as well. This loss created an echo chamber within the leadership so loud that by the time they were asking themselves why they kept losing such good talent, the bottom line was in freefall.

An alternative option would have been to have stayed and tried to act more like the men around us to convince leadership to move us up the ladder. But becoming anything other than what we authentically were wasn't something we were willing to do. Frankly, it shouldn't be something that *any* corporate woman should have to do to progress in leadership roles.

I often see women who, as they try to carve out a space for themselves, feel compelled to mirror their male counterparts. They adopt the attire, the demeanor, and even the communication style traditionally associated with men. Sure, they might get a few nods at the meeting, but at what cost? It's like trading in a perfectly good pair of comfortable sneakers for a pair of stiff, new dress shoes that just don't fit right. Though I do understand that the goal here is to be taken seriously and have the same shot at positions as their male colleagues, this comes at the cost of authenticity and, ultimately, credibility.

For many of their male counterparts, aggression and assertiveness were part of their upbringing. But many women, who are often raised to be accommodating and agreeable above all else, find these traits less innate and less natural. This leaves them floundering when they try to mirror their male counterparts, which can be harmful to the woman's reputation.

The attributes that define a good leader, when exhibited by a man, are often perceived differently when demonstrated by a woman. In a *Harvard Business Review* article, it was found that "Managers use more positive words to describe men in performance reviews and more negative ones to describe women."[27] In addition, that same article goes on to say that, "Some studies have shown that women are more likely to receive vague feedback that is not connected to objectives or business outcomes, which is a disadvantage when women are competing for job opportunities, promotions, and rewards, and in terms of women's professional growth and identity."

The same assertiveness that earns a man the label of "strong leader" can, when exhibited by a woman, be misconstrued as bossiness. Or the willingness to engage in conflict, seen as a positive in male leaders, can be interpreted as aggressiveness when it comes from a female counterpart. Women leaders who are aware of this find themselves walking a tightrope, balancing their natural dispositions with the need to adapt to leadership stereotypes. It's a delicate act of managing one's behavior to ensure that assertiveness doesn't spill over into aggression, that

---

27 (Smith, 2018)

decisiveness doesn't alienate, and that strength is not mistaken for insensitivity.

The key to fixing the patriarchy doesn't lie in mirroring our male counterparts. Instead, it lies in being true to our strengths as women and using those strengths for the benefit of the company. In my case, I am not only a woman, but a British woman, which is a double whammy: I was raised to be polite above all else, which included not interrupting or speaking over another. In the beginning of my career, I found myself in a constant struggle to speak up and assert my presence in rooms where, if I wasn't careful, my voice could easily be drowned out.

As I navigated through the early stages of my career, I realized that the real challenge wasn't just about being heard. It was about leaning into my natural strengths and using them to become more effective. When I did manage to get the floor, I communicated professionally (and most politely, of course), and when I hadn't been heard, I followed up in writing, copying all those who I believed needed to hear my contribution. Over time, due to how effective I was and how highly my teams performed, mine was a voice that others increasingly sought to hear.

Now, don't get me wrong. This journey wasn't without its missteps. But eventually, I found my stride. Once I embraced my own style, it was like slipping into a pair of custom-made boots, perfect in fit and function. It became clear that the key to challenging the patriarchal system was not in mirroring it, but in presenting a formidable authentic alternative.

Single-Gendered Leadership Disconnects Consumers

In case I haven't given you enough motivation to fight the patriarchy, doing so makes good business sense as well.

Men, despite their best efforts and expertise, might struggle to fully grasp the intricate experiences and needs of their female consumers. Think about it: do you know what a gender other than your own wants out of a product? Do you *really* know? Or do you just assume based on your analytics (minus nuance) and your general understanding of that gender? This gap in understanding can lead to marketing strategies that, while well-intentioned, fail to truly speak to the customers they aim to reach.

We need leadership composed of both men and women to better connect with our customers.

All-male leadership teams may inadvertently miss out on golden opportunities for innovation. Women, with their lived experiences and unique perspectives, often see what others overlook. They can identify unmet needs or suggest product enhancements that could revolutionize the market. A male-dominated marketing team, for example, no matter how capable, might simply not see these avenues, leaving untapped potential on the table.

Then, there's the delicate matter of representation. The marketing world is rife with examples where attempts to connect with female and other minority audiences have spectacularly backfired. Such missteps can erode trust and alienate a significant portion of the market. Plus, they are just plain embarrassing! Customers today seek brands that understand them and reflect their realities as well as values. So, an all-male team, looking to target a largely female or even an equal gendered customer base, is a grave mistake.

This misalignment will seep into the very fabric of the company's relationship with its customers. Women are known for their brand loyalty, but this loyalty is earned through a sense of kinship and understanding. When companies miss the mark, brand loyalty is compromised and very difficult to get back.

In today's world, where diversity and corporate responsibility are benchmarks for excellence, a glaring gender gap in management can (and eventually will) hurt a company's reputation. It raises questions about the company's commitment to truly understanding and valuing its diverse customer base. And today's customers are more observant and vocal than ever, thanks to social media. They are quick to notice and call out disparities, leading to a public relations challenge that no amount of damage control can easily fix.

Which is why the path to sustainable success for any company is paved with diversity within leadership.

When You Are a Leader Dealing with the Patriarchy

For women leaders, facing the patriarchy in the corporate world feels like trying to dance a waltz while others are aggressively breakdancing around you. This environment, dominated by traditional masculine styles of leadership, presents unique opportunities for women to differentiate themselves.

Just as men in leadership roles have long been encouraged to leverage their strengths, women too should embrace this approach. Women leaders have a reservoir of unique abilities, often rooted in emotional intelligence (EQ), which can be a distinct advantage in the business world. By confidently navigating the corporate terrain with these inherent strengths, women can effectively counterbalance the aggressive "breakdance" of the traditional corporate patriarchy with their own style of "waltz," creating a harmonious and impactful leadership presence.

These strengths—sensitivity, empathy, and a nuanced understanding of the human condition, in addition to their myriad professional skills—are increasingly being recognized as vital to organizational success. In a business landscape where relationships, team dynamics, and employee engagement are pivotal, these traits can be game changers. They enable a deeper connection with teams, foster a more collaborative environment, and lead to more sustainable and holistic business solutions.

However, leveraging these strengths isn't always straightforward. It requires a degree of courage, especially in the face of traditional corporate norms that may undervalue or misunderstand these qualities. My personal experience with introducing personal mastery and personal development workshops in my organization is a testament to this. Despite initial resistance and skepticism, with some of the participants even trying to avoid the training (who wants to sit through hours of training when you are busy!), the impact was undeniable. Both men and women recognized the value these courses brought to their personal and professional growth and, by extension, to their teams.

I remember the head of Project Management in one company who was likable and reserved. She was uncomfortable in the run-up to a personal mastery course, asking politely if she could be excused. I reiterated the reasons why I thought this work would help take each individual and the entire team to a new level of personal growth and fulfillment which would ultimately lead to much better collective results. The "pursuit of excellence" argument persuaded her to join, but she remained skeptical and out of her comfort zone. And she wasn't the only one. Many people feel that soft skills in business aren't required, but the truth is, if you take the time to learn them, they will make a *huge* difference in your career.

The workshop spanned three days, and I kept a close eye on her progress. After day one, she was still uncomfortable. At the end of day two, she looked more at ease and had adopted a more open and curious posture. At the end of day three, she approached me to say she had applied some of the lessons from the workshop discussions at home and was "blown away" by the positive response from her husband and daughter. She said to me that she was thrilled that she could truly say that the course had opened her eyes to a simple, authentic way to connect with her family, and that at least it had had a positive impact on her personal life. Needless to say, only a few days later, she laughingly reported that the impact on her professional life was just as powerful!

By leaning into these strengths, all leaders can affect meaningful change within their organizations. They can shift perceptions, break down barriers, and contribute to a more empathetic, aware, and ultimately successful business environment. Embracing your strengths as a woman in leadership doesn't mean you have to adopt the "I can do it all in heels" mantra (unless, of course, you really can—in which case, kudos!). It is more about recognizing that your approach to leadership might be different.

This journey is, of course, packed with a set of nuanced considerations. Women in leadership or aspiring to be leaders are often scrutinized through a lens tainted with gender biases. These biases can manifest in stereotypes, labeling women as overly emotional or talkative, for example.

To navigate this landscape effectively, we have to be aware of these stereotypes and consciously steer clear of actions that could reinforce them. *Professionalism is the guiding principle here, and it extends beyond just work performance.* It encompasses attire, behavior, and social interactions within the workplace. This doesn't imply a rigid, impersonal demeanor; instead, the goal is to maintain a balance where interactions are respectful, considerate, and appropriate.

Addressing the patriarchy in the corporate world starts with a commitment to personal development and personal mastery, both for male and female leaders. It requires deep introspection and a readiness to stretch beyond comfort zones. For male leaders, this often means recognizing and unlearning previously unconscious biases, developing greater empathy for diverse experiences and perspectives, and fostering an inclusive leadership style that prioritizes equity and respect. When people in leadership positions commit to this journey, the impact is significant. It creates an environment where both men and women can thrive, where their talents are recognized, and their contributions valued.

But none of this can happen unless all of us—men and women—are willing to acknowledge and watch out for patriarchal practices. We have to speak up when they happen. And we have to stop avoiding this conversation. If we don't, no individual or company will escape the negative effects of the patriarchy.

Chapter Wrap Up

Pretending the patriarchy isn't a problem won't make it better. Keep in mind that:

- While the patriarchy has gotten better, it is still present and hurts companies and individuals.
- Defining and acknowledging the negative effects of the patriarchy can be difficult, but they cannot be ignored.
- Acting outside of our authentic selves to mirror the leadership norms isn't the answer.
- Single-gendered approaches hinder companies and can distance them from their customer base.
- Lean into your inherent strengths to become the leader you were meant to be, even if they are different from those of people around you. Your strengths will make you an authentic and unique leader.

Chapter 10:

Adopt Personal Mastery

When was the last time you doubted yourself? Was it today, yesterday, or last week? We all doubt ourselves, probably more than we should. Imposter syndrome is something each of us silently battles at one point or another, especially when we realize that we are each simply striving to do the best we can in this world. Our minds are wired to focus more on our failures and shortcomings than on our successes. This negative bias can be amplified by societal and cultural norms that set high, sometimes unattainable, standards of perfection.

Personal mastery is the antidote to imposter syndrome. In the light of self-awareness, the fears that fuel our self-doubt begin to lose their grip. An individual grounded in personal mastery recognizes their abilities and understands that proficiency is not about being perfect; it's about learning, growing, and occasionally laughing when you trip over yourself.

I bet you can think of someone in your life who has focused on personal development and is visibly evolving. Their actions are deliberate and intentional. Their challenges are met with steady resolve. Their confidence, quiet yet solid, stems from an authentic understanding of their own value and capabilities. Does anyone you know come to mind?

Each of us knows a person or two who have shown up in this manner, as their best selves. Maybe we even look up to them or wish we could be more like them. Yet, it can still be difficult for us to figure out how to achieve this higher state.

To help you, here are the six principles of personal mastery I adhere to.

6 Principles of Personal Mastery

These principles are the distilled essence of hard-earned wisdom, gleaned over years of leading teams, making tough decisions, working on myself, reading books, attending courses, and facing challenges head-on. I hope my hard-earned lessons can give you the cheat code you need to commence your own personal mastery journey.

1. Commitment Is Key to Personal Mastery

Commitment, in its truest form, is a mark of class and distinction in both personal and professional worlds. An executive at American Express once said, "Commitment is what transforms a promise into reality. It is the words that speak boldly of your intentions, and the actions which speak louder than words. Commitment is the stuff character is made of, the power to change the face of things, it is the daily triumph of integrity over skepticism."[28]

---

28 (Neeld, 1990)

I believe she is right. Commitment is the bedrock you need when it comes to personal mastery. When you make a promise to be somewhere, honoring that promise by being punctual is a tangible manifestation of your commitment. Similarly, when you commit to completing a task, following through to its completion reflects your reliability and integrity. These actions, though seemingly small, are significant indicators of your character.

Now don't get me wrong, I *know* life is full of unexpected challenges which might make it difficult to keep some of your commitments. But really, what shows your commitment is how you handle the curveballs. Commitment is not just about adhering to promises, it is also about managing expectations. If you are running late for a meeting (life happens, right?), the key is to give a quick heads-up to those waiting for you. If you're in a spot where you can't keep a commitment, just be upfront about it. Reach out as soon as you can, explain the situation, and work out a plan B. By informing the affected parties when the unexpected occurs, by re-negotiating your agreement and setting the expectations for what you can do in the situation, you *are* keeping your commitment to those parties.

Don't forget to include yourself in your commitments. We need to commit to our ideas, our goals, and our words. And this often requires a change in language. In a meeting, instead of saying, "What if we maybe try this," try saying, "I request we . . ." This language is more clear and more committed to the idea! Watch how the dynamics shift when you commit to your own words. It often leads to more respect and credibility from your peers.

You can make other changes that make you sound more confident and committed as well. Such as changing "I probably should . . ." to "I commit to . . ." or replacing "I have to . . ." with "I get to . . ." This simple swap transforms a task from a burden to an opportunity, and it often changes your internal approach to the task.

The way we talk to ourselves and to others shapes our reality, our self-perception, and our approach to challenges. You are in charge of your own experience, and the sooner you embrace and internalize this, the sooner you'll see tangible changes in your results in all aspects of your life. This all happens through commitment, and it is a huge key to personal mastery that many people underestimate.

2. Circumstance Isn't King

In school, we all heard the famous quote from Charles R. Swindoll: "10% of life is what happens to you, and the other 90% is how you react to it."[29] Yet sometimes, I think we tend to forget this as adults.

Personal mastery, at its heart, is about recognizing and embracing your personal power. No matter the circumstance, you have the power to choose how you react to any given situation. This is so important! Especially if you are in your career and you have to deal with a toxic situation. You can still choose how you react.

---

29 (Swindoll, n.d.)

It was George Bernard Shaw, the Irish playwright and political activist, who said, "People are always blaming their circumstances for what they are. I don't believe in circumstances. The people who get on in this world are the people who get up and look for the circumstances they want, and if they can't find them, make them."[30] Think about the leaders you admire. Did they simply go along with their circumstance? Or did they keep pushing until they *made* the circumstance they needed and wanted?

Viktor Frankl, a renowned psychiatrist and Holocaust survivor, witnessed and endured the horrors of concentration camps during World War II. These experiences profoundly shaped his psychological theories, and in his work, *Man's Search for Meaning*[31], Frankl recounts the grim reality of life in the camps. He highlights the unimaginable suffering, brutality, and the constant shadow of death. In the face of all that, he outlines his perspective on freedom and willpower.

He saw himself and his fellow inmates as the true free individuals, despite their physical confinement. In his view, they retained the most crucial freedom of all—the freedom to choose their attitude and response to their suffering. The Nazis, on the other hand, were prisoners in Frankl's eyes. They had surrendered their free will to a heinous system, becoming cogs in a machine of hatred and oppression. They were bound by an ideology that stripped them of their humanity and individual moral judgment.

---

30 (Shaw, n.d.)
31 (Frankl, 2011)

While we cannot control every aspect of our lives, we have the ultimate control over how we respond to our circumstances.

Falling into a victim mentality is like getting stuck in quicksand. The more you wallow in thoughts like "I can't" or "I'm not good enough" or "nobody cares," the deeper you sink into a mediocre drift. Which is where potential goes to retire early and opportunities wave goodbye. *It's the unintended consequence of handing over the steering wheel of your life to circumstance, instead of navigating your own course.*

Our circumstances do not dictate our lives. We have to be proactive. Are you waiting for things to happen, passively letting the currents of circumstance carry you along? Or are you actively looking forward, being strategic and creative in your approach? The difference between these two outlooks on life can mean the difference between stagnation and growth.

3. Differentiate Between Perfection and Excellence

Though personal mastery might suggest a quest for perfection, in reality, it's far from it. The goal is actually to strive for excellence, which is a significantly more attainable goal.

You do not need perfection to happen for excellence to occur. Excellence is about striving to do your best within the realm of your abilities. It's focused on continuous improvement and growth. Perfection is the pursuit of a flawless and faultless outcome, often an idealized or unrealistic standard.

When something doesn't work out, it's not a cue to indulge in self-blame. It's an opportunity to learn and move forward. When coming out of hibernation, the hungry bear does not berate itself when it can't find food in the first place it looks. It simply moves on to the next spot. If we encounter setbacks, we should not self-criticize or give up. Instead, we should reassess, learn, and adjust our strategies. Just like the bear, we should recognize that not every effort will yield immediate success, and that's perfectly okay. It's part of the natural process of exploration and growth. Moving on to the next opportunity with the lessons learned is a healthier and more productive way to approach challenges.

Leaders who chase perfection often become risk averse. Their fear of failure makes them close themselves off to new ideas and innovative approaches, ironically stifling the very success they seek to achieve. They tend to be reactive, operating out of fear, and they often find their window of opportunity and enjoyment narrowing. Their leadership can lack excitement, creativity, and a sense of achievement, both for themselves and their teams.

In contrast, those leaders who pursue excellence are proactive. They embrace risk, innovation, and learning, creating an environment of excitement and possibility. They strive for excellence and are constantly seeking new ways to innovate, recognizing that innovation is key to staying relevant. They understand that knowledge and skills are not static. As a result, the pursuit of excellence fosters an organizational culture that is forward-thinking, curious, adaptive, and energized.

Ask yourself—between those two descriptors, which type of leader do you want to be?

4. Be Open and Flexible and Go for the Win/Win

When faced with questions or challenges about a project, how do you respond? Do you instinctively become defensive, seeing the question as a challenge to your authority? Or do you choose to listen, recognizing it as an opportunity for collaboration and improvement?

Your reaction is indicative of your overall approach to leadership and control. Often, those who are constantly striving to exert control find themselves losing their grip over their team and projects. The more they try to micromanage and dictate every single detail, the more resistance and disengagement they encounter from their team.

The real secret to effective leadership and maintaining control lies in the ability to let go of the minutiae. Leadership isn't about commanding every aspect; it's about guiding and shaping the direction. By shifting focus from micromanaging to sharing a clear vision and objectives, you empower your team. Which creates an environment where team members feel valued and responsible for their contributions.

That way, when a question or challenge arises, it becomes a collaborative effort to refine and improve, rather than a tug-of-war over control. Listening to your team and considering their perspectives enhances the project and solidifies your role as a leader who values input and fosters a culture of open communication. Being open is not a passive state; it's an active skill that requires intentional effort and practice.

In my career, one of the stark differences between myself and some leaders I encountered was our perspective on success. While they viewed it as a win-lose race, I always believed in lifting the entire company. I continually tried to be open and flexible about all ideas and perspectives, because any one of them could bring us to the excellence I wanted from myself and my team.

Adopting this mindset can be challenging. It might not always yield immediate benefits, and it certainly requires bravery. But you will find that becoming open and flexible actually gives you more ideas, information, and connections than being the closed and unapproachable leader ever would.

5. Be Accepting

Have you ever watched a scene in a movie where two characters are fighting, and one is shouting while the other remains calm? At that moment, who do you think has the power?

When someone angrily shouts at us, many of us want to shout right back. It's a natural reaction. But if you can remain calm, and don't take their outburst personally, you effectively defuse the situation. By standing firm in your beliefs yet allowing others the space to express their emotions, you subtly remove the impact and power from their anger.

Being the "accountable adult in the room" means resisting the urge to play the victim or shout back at the person pointing the finger. Even when it's tempting to become defensive or lash out. Instead, the goal is to accept that this *is* truly how they feel in the moment and to concentrate on what you can control—your actions, responses, and decisions—to improve the situation.

The moment you catch yourself focusing on who is to blame, pause and refocus. Ask yourself, "What role can I play in resolving this issue? What responsibility can I take?" This shift from blame to accountability moves you from a position of passivity to one of empowerment, where you are an active participant in finding solutions. Adopting an accepting and accountable attitude is powerful in any environment, be it professional or personal, and it positions you as a leader in these challenging moments.

6. To Achieve Personal Power, Let Go of Resistance

Resistance, at its core, is rooted in fear and perceived risk. Imagine a line. On one end, you have your comfort zone. On the other, you have fear and risk. As you move along the line, you edge closer to what feels like dangerous territory, triggering your brain's instinctive response to perceived threats.

Our brains don't like us moving toward our fears.

Which is why many of us get stuck in our comfort zones. We cling to routines and known paths, often because stepping outside of them feels daunting or even threatening. But, this comfort zone, while cozy and reassuring, is also a place where growth is limited. Breaking out of this cycle means realizing that you are in control of your own experience.

Embracing personal power is a choice. Power is not handed to you; you must actively choose it. When you confront something you have been resisting, and consciously let it go, you effectively strip it of its power over you and, in turn, empower yourself.

We all have areas of resistance, and it's natural. Personal mastery helps us to acknowledge these resistances, understand their root causes, and then consciously work to let them go.

7. Where to Start Your Personal Mastery Journey

I hope these principles give you a good baseline for personal mastery. But I'd like to provide you with a bit more insight if you are new to this journey and want to learn more about raising your game.

A great starting point could be participating in workshops, consulting with personal development coaches, enrolling in courses, or diving into books that focus on self-improvement. The key is to find resources that resonate with you personally. Remember, personal mastery doesn't occur in isolation. It often requires external input and guidance.

Which is why I believe a workshop can be particularly eye-opening. The experience of being in a shared space, learning and growing with others, is invaluable. If you find a program or workshop that speaks to you, don't stop there. Bring your team along! I've done this numerous times throughout my career, and the benefits have always been extensive. You'll find that many leaders you admire, including Fortune 500 CEOs, have become deeply engaged in this kind of work and have extended it to their teams and peers. They recognize the value of it, and because they prioritize it, they create high-performing teams.

Introducing your team to personal mastery concepts isn't always straightforward. Carving out time for workshops, overcoming skepticism, and putting your reputation on the line can be challenging. But I promise, it is worth the effort. Before involving my team, I always vetted the course personally. I wanted to be sure the workshop aligned with the values and behavioral principles I had outlined for my team. Afterall, I wouldn't ask my team to do anything I wouldn't do myself, and neither should you!

To this day, when reconnecting with colleagues, we rarely discuss product results or revenue achievement successes. Instead, our conversations revolve around personal growth and career development. The workshops and personal mastery work we did together have acted as catalysts for each of us, sparking significant changes in individual behaviors (both at home and at work) and in the collective dynamics and successes of our teams.

As you tackle imposter syndrome in your day-to-day lives, remember, personal mastery is your antidote. When you engage in this kind of work, you are fundamentally reshaping how you think, interact, and respond to opportunities and challenges. Investing in this personal and professional development for you and your team paves the way to a significantly more fulfilling and impactful career and to leaving a legacy that you can be proud of.

Chapter Wrap Up

To nix imposter syndrome through personal mastery, remember:

- Personal mastery is the antidote for imposter syndrome.
- An individual grounded in personal mastery recognizes their strengths and their weaknesses.
- Personal mastery, at its heart, is about embracing your personal power.
- You do not need perfection to happen for excellence to occur, but you do need a mindset of continuous improvement to achieve excellence.
- Those who are trying to exert control over others are those who find themselves with the least of it. Focusing on team growth instead of task management helps avoid this.
- Stand firm in your beliefs, but also be willing to allow others to express theirs.
- Being stuck in your comfort zone is limiting. Break out of it to take yourself, your team, and your company to new heights, even if this means you experience a few failures along the way.
- Start your personal mastery journey with a workshop (then take your team!).

Chapter 11:

Get in Alignment

The stereotypically difficult leaders we so often encounter are misaligned.

They have polished shoes and rehearsed smiles. But sadly, they aren't authentic. They speak in buzzwords and jargon, often saying a lot without really saying anything meaningful. Their speeches are peppered with phrases like "synergy" and "paradigm shifts," but these words are usually more for show than substance. Especially if they are charismatic (which they often are). They might know how to light up a room and make a group of people feel they are a part of something big and exciting. But their follow-through on bold promises, and their understanding of the nitty-gritty details of their team's daily challenges, is where things start to get murky.

They are disconnected. Their public persona and their actual leadership effectiveness are not aligned. This is demoralizing for the teams who follow them. Teams thrive on authenticity and consistency, and when these are missing, it's like trying to build a house on shifting sands.

Can you think of a leader like this? How did they make you feel? Did you trust anything they said?

When you witness this kind of dissonance, where leaders promise the moon but barely deliver a rock, it's a classic case of misalignment. These leaders are not in harmony with their words. There's a glaring gap between what they say and what they do, and it's as obvious as a neon sign in a dark alley. Once you've seen this kind of performance, you can't unsee it. And it means in the next all-hands meeting—as the leader in question gives their motivational speech—you are likely to be internally rolling your eyes.

How Do You Know If You Are in Alignment?

If leaders are talking the talk, but not walking the walk, their words and actions are not aligned. We have all experienced this type of leader. And none of us want to be them. But to make sure you can walk the walk *and* talk the talk, you have to identify whether you are aligned or inauthentic.

How consistent is your sense of self and your actions? Are you the same person no matter the situation? Or do you become someone else when tensions get high?

Lack of authenticity occurs when there is a mismatch between your words and actions. And it is perceived as artificial and untruthful. The worst thing you can do, especially as a leader, is be inconsistent—presenting one persona one day and an entirely different one the next. Losing sight of your personal north star is too easy.

When you are caught up in the whirlwind of deadlines, presentations, and family commitments, your north star (that's your core values) can get muddied. Especially when you hop from task to task, put out fires all day, and are regularly under pressure. When this happens for an extended period of time, we start running on autopilot and stop checking in with ourselves.

When you are not aligned with your true self, it might affect the way you interact with others. You might react in ways that are out of character, leading to misunderstandings or conflicts that could have been avoided. Don't wait until a misstep has escalated into a significant problem. Instead, regularly check in with yourself. Are your actions and decisions reflective of who you truly are and what you stand for? Are you being the person, and the leader, that you aspire to be?

If the answer is no, recalibrate.

Maintain Alignment through Self-Check-Ins

To stay aligned, you need to embrace mindfulness and make it a consistent practice. Even when chaos reigns, this should be a daily practice. Without it, you won't get the clarity you need to make decisions that are effective and true to who you are. Many people I've spoken with couldn't believe they put up with toxic treatment from a past boss or peer, and some only realized how bad that treatment was once they left their situation. They didn't check in on themselves, which left them blinded and unprepared and made it difficult to stand up for their personal values.

Think of your day-to-day life. How often do you pause and ask yourself if what you're doing aligns with your core values? Are your daily actions and decisions a reflection of what you truly stand for, or are they just reactions to the demands placed upon you? When you think strategically about your own alignment, you give yourself the space to stop and say, "This situation isn't for me" or to say, "This situation is for me, and I want more of it."

Mindfulness can look different for everyone. For some, it might be meditation; for others, it might be yoga, running, or walking. Connecting with nature, feeling the rhythm of your steps, or even walking your dog can be grounding. It doesn't matter what you do as long as you take time to be in silence and let your mind consider your own life. These moments of introspection allow you to check in with yourself, to ensure that you are still aligned with your values and goals.

During these moments, try to leave the headphones behind. Allow yourself the space to just be with your thoughts. Without the constant stream of music or podcasts, it might feel initially like your thoughts are racing uncontrollably. But given time, and with a bit of practice in stilling your mind, you'll find that you can start to untangle and make sense of these thoughts, as your inner voice becomes louder and clearer. And it doesn't have to be walking; it could be anything that refuels you and feels comfortable. It might be sitting quietly with a morning coffee, journaling, or simply staring out the window at the start or end of your day. The key is to find what works for you, something that allows you to pause and reflect amidst the daily hustle.

These practices serve as a way to recalibrate and realign when the noise of the outside world becomes too distracting.

Neglecting these practices can lead to a gradual, often unnoticed drift off course. Over time, this misalignment manifests in various forms of discomfort or dissatisfaction. You might feel uneasy about a business transaction, a conversation with a colleague, or even the state of your personal relationships. No matter how hard we try, there will be moments in each of our lives where we step out of alignment. No one is immune to it; all of us, at one point or another, find ourselves straying from our path. The sense of unease is a signal—it's your inner self trying to alert you that you are moving away from who you truly are and what you stand for. Your inner self will try to communicate with you, sometimes subtly, other times forcefully.

The trick is catching when it happens and doing something to correct it.

We often prioritize everything and everyone else over taking a moment for ourselves. It is easy to get caught up in the day's chores and the endless to-do lists. But maintaining your alignment is an essential part of your well-being and effectiveness as a leader and individual contributor. It *needs* to be prioritized.

How Often?

A good friend of mine—a remarkable individual with a PhD, a successful book, and positions on various boards—refused to go even one day without checking in with herself. While we were on a cabin retreat with friends, she excused herself for a moment with a cheerful, "Hold on, girls, I'll be with you in a few minutes!" and took the time for her meditation practice.

She is committed to self-alignment, regardless of the setting or company. And her success is the result of being tuned in to who she is at her core.

The goal isn't to carve out large chunks of your day; rather, it's about consistency and quality of the time spent. Even just five to ten minutes a day can make a significant difference. If finding time daily is a challenge, try finding an hour once a week to check in. Something is always better than nothing when it comes to self-reflection. But for it to be truly beneficial, it needs to be a regular practice.

What Should I Ask Myself?

Begin by setting purpose-driven goals. Remember, these goals shouldn't be a source of additional stress. Instead, think of them as gentle guideposts.

Ask yourself the following questions:

- Am I satisfied with where I am in my life right now?
- Is there an aspect I'd like to improve?
- If there is, what small thing can I do to make progress towards that goal?

This self-dialogue should feel natural and easy. It's a conversation with yourself about your current life and what small beneficial changes you want to incorporate into your daily routine to improve it. If you become critical of yourself, stop! Analyzing and dissecting everything you did wrong isn't the point. The only goal of these conversations is to pause, take stock, and realign yourself if necessary. There should be no judgment or self-criticism involved, only constructive self-assessment.

The Desire Map, written by Danielle LaPorte, offers an approach to creating goals that have soul. On the back cover, it reads, "Knowing how you want to feel is the most important clarity you can have. Generating those feelings is the most powerful thing you can do with your life."[32] Accompanying the book is a workbook that guides you through a journey of self-discovery across different aspects of your life with the goal of helping you tune in to your true self and ask fundamental questions like, "Am I where I want to be?" and "Do I feel good about these areas of my life?" I recommend it if you are unsure of what your larger goals in life might be.

Once you know what you deeply desire, you can use the questions above to check in on your progress.

This process is so powerful, but so few people do it. They get tied up with getting the next thing they want and forget that before they can be truly happy, they have to be in alignment. If you get this emotional side of your life right, everything else falls more readily into place. It simplifies decision making and prioritization, and it gives you clarity on what makes you happy. At the end of the day, isn't happiness what we are all chasing?

---

32 (Laporte, 2014)

Of course, happiness means different things to different people. If you can pinpoint what happiness means to you, you have won half the battle. The rest of your decisions, big and small, start aligning naturally with the pursuit of *your* happiness.

Clarity Is Your Shield Against Toxicity

By now, I think you'll have realized that all this advice on alignment, and all the other advice throughout this book, boils down to this: *you need to get crystal clear about who you are, what you stand for, and what your goals are.*

When it comes to your career, you are in the driver's seat. No one else is going to steer your life for you. I've seen too many employees in the corporate world who, without even realizing it, hand over the keys to their happiness, progress, and success to someone else. But you need to keep a firm grip on that steering wheel. To stay on course, you've got to do the groundwork. Figure out what you stand for and then chase those dreams relentlessly.

I firmly believe that this is the secret recipe for happiness, confidence, self-worth, mutually respectful relationships, and your very own version of success.

We can be so picky when it comes to what we wear, who our friends are, and where we eat. But we aren't typically as picky when it comes to our job. Our careers should give us a return, not just in terms of salary and benefits, but in terms of meaning and fulfillment. It's time to be just as selective about these things because, at the end of the day, you deserve nothing less.

Chapter Wrap Up

The more aligned you are, the better you will lead. Keep in mind:

- Difficult leaders are typically misaligned.
- Lack of authenticity occurs when there is a mismatch between your words and your actions. Check in with yourself to be sure the two are reflective of each other.
- Without inner reflection, we risk drifting off our path and becoming misaligned.
- Make mindfulness part of your daily routine and ditch the headphones during this time.
- Include helpful self-dialogue during these mindfulness sessions; anything else isn't helpful and isn't the point of these moments.
- Remember, clarity on your alignment acts as a shield against veering off your path. You'll find that, when difficult or boundary-breaking situations occur, you'll have a clearer picture of what to do if you are aligned with your inner self.

A Final Word

Whether you are already in a leadership position, or you hope to gain one, you now have the tools you need to become an evolved and impactful leader.

Many start their careers full of optimism and enthusiasm, only to see that spark dimmed over time, crushed by the poor leadership they encounter. The corporate world doesn't need more leaders who lead with micromanagement and inconsistency or even fear and intimidation. What it needs are leaders who recognize and value the humanity in their teams. Leaders who understand that their true legacy lies in the growth and development of their people.

As you step forward in your career and life, remember that you deserve an environment that aligns with your values, where you are respected, and where your contributions are valued. You deserve leaders that inspire rather than drain, and you have the potential to be the kind of leader yourself who truly makes a difference.

This book was inspired by a deep-seated need to share what I've learned. I have coached, given advice, and provided workshops on leadership, because poor leadership is such a common issue many struggle with in today's world. Through my coaching, both formal and informal, I've seen the moment of realization in people's eyes time and again—the understanding that they deserve more and don't have to settle for a toxic work environment or a bad boss. I've talked to many who found subpar leadership to be the norm, as I once did, and I helped them see that they don't have to tolerate this passion-draining, soul-crushing experience. Watching people secure roles that bring them happiness and fulfillment, roles that support them to become the leaders they have always wanted to be, is incredible. I hope this book helps you on that journey.

The strategies and insights shared here are tools for you to build a leadership style that resonates with your true self. As you close this book, my hope is that you feel equipped and inspired to be the leader who makes a real difference. If even one reader takes these principles to heart and applies them to their leadership journey, every word I have written will have been worthwhile.

Remember, it's common to feel trapped in the corporate world, believing there is no escape from the status quo. But through this book, I hope I have shown you that change is possible. If you ever find yourself wondering, "Is this it? Is this all I can expect?" know that the answer is a resounding "No." You have the power to change your situation and to be a catalyst for a positive workplace.

The corporate world is teeming with leadership of all kinds. *It's time for the good leaders to outnumber the bad.* The change starts with you.

Bibliography

(n.d.). From Lassoism: https://lassoism.com/Ted-Lasso-quote.
php?id=65

(n.d.). From New York Times: https://www.nytimes.
com/2015/06/27/business/dealbook/the-bad-behavior-
of-visionary-leaders.html

Aragao, C. (2023, March 1). From Pew Research Center: https://
www.pewresearch.org/short-reads/2023/03/01/gender-
pay-gap-facts/#:~:text=In%202022%2C%20women%20
earned%20an,80%25%20as%20much%20as%20men.

Blanchard, K. (2017). *The One Minute Manager.* William
Morrow.

Brown, B. (2018, October 15). From Brene Brown: https://
brenebrown.com/articles/2018/10/15/clear-is-kind-
unclear-is-unkind/

DiSC. (n.d.). From DiSC: https://www.discprofile.com/what-is-
disc/history-of-disc

Falk, S. (2023, March 1). From CNBC: https://www.cnbc.
com/2023/03/01/psychology-expert-shares-toxic-signs-
of-a-highly-insecure-person-and-how-to-deal-with-

them.html#:~:text=While%20feeling%20insecure%20
is%20natural,nasty%20or%20display%20abusive%20
behaviors.

Frankl, V. (2011). *Man's Search for Meaning.* Rider.

Gallup. (n.d.). From Gallup: https://www.gallup.com/
services/182138/state-american-manager.aspx

Goffee, R., & Jones, G. (2013, May). From Harvard Business
Review: https://hbr.org/2013/05/creating-the-best-
workplace-on-earth

Half, R. (2023, May 26). From Robert Half: https://
www.roberthalf.com/us/en/insights/career-
development/10-quotes-to-inspire-active-
listening#:~:text=%E2%80%9COf%20all%20the%20
skills%20of,of%20unseen%20problems%20and%20
opportunities.%E2%80%9D

Harter, J. (2022, April 25). From Gallup: https://www.gallup.
com/workplace/391922/employee-engagement-slump-
continues.aspx

Hoffman, B. (2013). *American Icon.* Crown Currency.

Indeed. (2023, September 22). From Indeed: https://www.
indeed.com/career-advice/career-development/guiding-
principles-examples#:~:text=Guiding%20principles%20
help%20managers%20and,satisfaction%20and%20
foster%20professional%20success.

Jeffers, S. (2006). *Feel the Fear and Do It Anyway.* Ballantine Books.

Laporte, D. (2014). *The Desire Map.* Sounds True Adult.

Lofgren, J. (2021, May 17). From Forbes: https://www.forbes.com/sites/forbescoachescouncil/2021/05/17/the-role-that-boundaries-play-in-leadership-growth/?sh=33c32d347066

MindTools. (n.d.). From Mind Tools: https://www.mindtools.com/au7v71d/the-johari-window

Neeld, E. H. (1990). *Seven Choices.* Centerpoint Press.

Nolan, T. (n.d.). From Gallup: https://www.gallup.com/workplace/232955/no-employee-benefit-no-one-talking.aspx

PwC. (2023, June 19). From PwC Global: https://www.pwc.com/gx/en/issues/workforce/hopes-and-fears.html

Salesforce. (n.d.). From Salesforce Research: https://a.sfdcstatic.com/content/dam/www/ocms-backup/assets/pdf/misc/salesforce-research-2017-workplace-equality-and-values-report.pdf

Saujani, R. (2019). *Brave, Not Perfect.* Crown Currency.

Shaw, G. B. (n.d.). From Forbes: https://www.forbes.com/quotes/3370/

Smith, D. (2018). From Harvard Business Review: https://hbr.
org/data-visuals/2018/05/managers-use-more-positive-
words-to-describe-men-in-performance-reviews-and-
more-negative-ones-to-describe-women

Swindoll, C. R. (n.d.). From Goodreads: https://www.goodreads.
com/author/quotes/5139.Charles_R_Swindoll

Tenney, M. (n.d.). From Business Leadership Today:
https://businessleadershiptoday.com/what-
is-the-impact-of-servant-leadership-in-an-
organization/#:~:text=increase%20psychological%20
safety.-,Performance,that%20they%20can%20perform%-
20better.

Tenney, M. (2014). *Serve to Be Great.* Wiley.

Unknown. (2023, July 11). *Student Wellness.* From
University of Guelth: https://wellness.uoguelph.
ca/news/boundaries-vs-controlling-behaviours-
whats-difference#:~:text=A%20boundary%20is%20
something%20we,you%20want%20them%20to%20do.

Wargo, E. (2006, July 1). From Association for Psychological
Science: https://www.psychologicalscience.org/observer/
how-many-seconds-to-a-first-impression

Zak, P. (2017). From Harvard Business Review: https://hbr.
org/2017/01/the-neuroscience-of-trust

Acknowledgments

I wouldn't have had the career I enjoyed or be close to where I am today without the unstinting love and support of my husband, Peter. From the moment we married, we approached our lives as a mutually supportive partnership, with no rules as to who performed which role to advance the "Good Ship Jackson." I'm so thankful that we viewed our lives the same way and through the same prisms, approaching opportunities that came our way as part of one big adventure.

As our two daughters, Amy and Katie, grew, they thankfully adopted a similar worldview. Consequently, our family of four became my, and all of our, safe haven from which to explore the world and launch every ambition. My daughters have many impressive accomplishments, but the one that I'm most happy about and proud of is that they are wonderful women, clear-eyed and in alignment with their values and what they stand for.

Of course, no acknowledgement would be complete without thanking my mum and dad for their love and encouragement throughout my childhood and studies in Scotland and career in Europe and then in America. My mum provided me with the powerful weapon of having someone in my corner, no matter what! She had an unwavering (and very biased) belief in me that I wish was everyone on the planet's birthright! There's no question that my self-esteem stemmed from a certainty of being loved. My dad instilled in me the absolute belief that women and men should have equal opportunity, and as an intellectual and university professional himself, he role-modeled the benefits of education and critical thinking.

Throughout my career, I encountered many bad bosses and toxic individuals, and I'd like to acknowledge the impact they made on me to become passionate about leadership. To develop my skills and put every effort into being the change I wanted to see, and ultimately to writing this book.

I am honored to say that friends have been a crucial source of support throughout my journey. From High School days, I'm still in touch with Julia Langlands and Yvonne Bland, now living in Scotland and Canada, and despite great distances I am so glad to say that we still travel to see each other. Every time we meet it's like no time has passed (they say that about real friends, don't they?). We act as soundboards and cheerleaders for each other as we share our disappointments, triumphs, and dreams.

From early American career days, the Women of Substance group (WOS) that we formed continues to be there for one another, always supporting and cheering each other on. Thank you to Cathy Holton, Tina Bain, Clair Bancino, Christina Norris, and Cristina Fuster. I'm strengthened by your support, and I continue to be inspired by each of you.

Among the excellent individuals I was privileged to get to know in my career, I'd like to call out Connie Tang, who was a colleague in California, who embodied all the characteristics I encourage within this book and more! Connie and I could not have physically looked more different, but we took to calling each other "twin" due to our uncanny tendency to finish each other's sentences. In many respects, she was a professional soulmate.

I'd like to thank Bert Crandell, who was a true leader. He was inspiring, transparent, trustworthy, and fair-minded. An impressive critical thinker, he encouraged all his direct reports, myself included, to be the best we could be and to collaborate in the pursuit of excellence. That was a team that I was thankful to have been a member of, an experience I look back on with a sense of achievement and pride, which was in no small part due to Bert's leadership. Bert had a major positive impact on me and my family. He was one of the few American colleagues my mum and dad got to meet, and they fully approved!

I'd like to thank a couple of members of that team, who continue to reaffirm my belief in humanity and whose values and ethics show up brightly in every interaction. Michael Norris and Cathy Holton were smart and trustworthy co-workers, great leaders to their teams, and remain friends to this day.

Other co-workers or direct reports who stood out for me are John Tolmie, Kristen Welch, Ros Simmons, Tyler Schuessler, Sinead Pollock, Gareth Hooper, Deb Bursley, Kristina Swift and Darla Brown, all of whom faced challenging situations together with me and never once dropped their personal standards, always behaving professionally, ethically, and with humanity.

A special thank you goes to Martha Borst whose personal development and self-mastery teachings had a huge impact on me and many of my teams. When I first attended one of Martha's public courses, so many things fell into place for me as I grappled with how to navigate leadership within the corporate world in a way that was true to me. Martha's inspiring work has helped me and so many more find our path and keep our resolve.

Thank you to Thomas Inserra who is leading the start-up Bank on whose Board I serve. Thomas has a sterling leadership track record and continues today by prioritizing culture and leadership development among the many tasks involved in establishing a new Bank.

And finally, a huge thank you to my good friend Audrey Sommerfeld, someone who has accompanied me through many ups and downs, and whose combined intellect, humanity, sense of humor and huge laugh make her one of the best people I know!

About the Author

As a leader, Janice has never believed in masks. She is the same person in the office as she is with friends and family. Born and educated in Scotland, she ventured into the hustle and bustle of London, weaving her career path in corporate marketing across Europe. She specialized in sales, marketing, and consumer products, and she rose up the corporate ladder. Then, in 1999, with the excitement of a new adventure in her daughter's eyes and the unyielding support of her husband, Janice and her tight-knit family stepped onto the shores of a new continent.

As her family navigated the unfamiliar terrains together, she continued up the ladder from Global Vice President to Chief Marketing Officer, President, Founder and Board Member of companies ranging from mid-size hyper-growth phenomena to billion-dollar behemoths. She has driven global product, brand, sales and marketing strategies and navigated the holistic responsibilities of Founder and Board Member. Her responsibilities have spanned 80+ global markets and over 450 staff. Janice speaks several languages and enjoys working across many cultures, striving in every one of her roles to be a servant to the people she leads.

Find Janice on LinkedIn and Facebook:
https://www.linkedin.com/in/janice-jackson-baa4291/
https://www.facebook.com/janice.jackson123